Total alles über Bayern

The Complete Bavaria

Wichtigste Datenquelle / Main data source:

Bayerisches Landesamt für Statistik und Datenverarbeitung

Dank an / Thanks to:

meine Familie / *my family*

sowie an / as well as to:
Magnus Bauch, Annika Biss, Joachim Cordshagen, Barbara Ettl, Bernhard Greller, Barbara Kink, Wolfgang Köbele, Klara Obermair, Dominik Prantl, Linda Schulz, Stephan Straßer, Irene Warres, Manu Winbeck.

Audi AG, Bayerischer Jagdverband e. V., Bayerisches Landesamt für Statistik und Datenverarbeitung, BMW AG, Haus der Bayerischen Geschichte

Auch bei Folio erschienen / Also available from Folio:

Total alles über Südtirol /
Alto Adige – Tutto di tutto /
The Complete South Tyrol
Hermann Gummerer / Franziska Hack
Infographics: no.parking

2. Auflage / edition 2013
ISBN 978-3-85256-607-8

Total alles über Österreich /
The Complete Austria
Sonja Franzke
Infographics: no.parking

1. Auflage / edition 2013
ISBN 978-3-85256-630-6

1. Auflage / edition 2014

Idee und Konzept / Idea & Concept: Hermann Gummerer, Franziska Maria Hack; no.parking
Translation into English: Jennifer Taylor
Lektorat / Proofreading: Franziska Maria Hack, Hermann Gummerer
Druckvorstufe / Prepress Service: Typoplus, Frangart
Grafik und Umbruch / Graphic design: no.parking, Vicenza
Printed in Italy
ISBN 978-3-85256-646-7

www.folioverlag.com

Martin Wittmann * Infographics: no.parking

In Zusammenarbeit mit / In collaboration with: Franziska Maria Hack & Hermann Gummerer

TOTAL ALLES ÜBER BAYERN

THE COMPLETE BAVARIA

Folio

Inhalt
Index

ABC

Der Autor / Martin Wittmann, 1979 im niederbayerischen Landshut geboren; Studium der Soziologie in München, unterbrochen von Aufenthalten in Melbourne und Barcelona. Nach dem Studium Hospitanz im Feuilleton der *Frankfurter Allgemeinen Zeitung* (FAZ), anschließend Volontariat an gleicher Stelle. Seit 2009 freier Journalist in München, in erster Linie tätig für die *Süddeutsche Zeitung*.

The author / Martin Wittmann, born 1979 in Landshut in Lower Bavaria; studied sociology in Munich, interrupted by stays abroad in Melbourne and Barcelona. After graduation, job shadowing in the features department of the *Frankfurter Allgemeine Zeitung* (FAZ), followed by a journalism traineeship there. Freelance journalist in Munich since 2009, working primarily for the *Süddeutsche Zeitung*.

Die Gestalterinnen / no.parking ist eine Agentur für Kommunikation und Gestaltung in Vicenza: Sabine Lercher, Caterina Romio, Elisa Dall'Angelo, Anna Saraconi, Gessica Padoan und Stefania Pellizzari switchen zwischen deutschem und italienischem Kulturraum hin und her und begreifen Design als etwas, das unser Leben schöner macht, nützlich ist und allen zugänglich sein sollte.

The graphic designers / no.parking is an agency for communication and design based in Vicenza. Sabine Lercher, Caterina Romio, Elisa Dall'Angelo, Anna Saraconi, Gessica Padoan and Stefania Pellizzari switch back and forth between the German and Italian cultural realms and view design as something that makes our lives more beautiful, something that is useful and should be accessible to all.
www.noparking.it

Die Co-Autoren / Franziska Maria Hack ist promovierte Sprachwissenschaftlerin und Lektorin im Folio Verlag.
Hermann Gummerer studierte Germanistik und Philosophie und ist Mitbegründer und Co-Verleger des Folio Verlags.

The co-authors / Franziska Maria Hack holds a PhD in linguistics and is an editor at Folio Verlag.
Hermann Gummerer studied German linguistics and literature and philosophy and is co-founder and co-owner of the Folio Verlag publishing company.

BAYERN EINMAL ANDERS BETRACHTET
A NEW WAY OF LOOKING AT BAVARIA

von oben / from above

im Profil / in profile

die Bewohner / the inhabitants

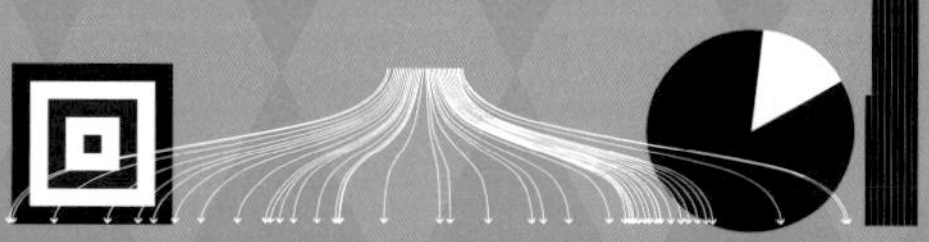

die Fakten / the facts

Grüß Gott!

Die Bayern sind ein wahrlich schwer zu verstehendes Volk, nicht nur ihrer Dialekte wegen. Auch ist in ihren Gesichtern kaum zu lesen. Manche Bayern gehen mit einem Lächeln durch's Leben – wohl, weil sich in ihrer Heimat der FCB auf den BMW reimt; weil die Polizisten hier seltener schießen als die Jäger; weil die Ärzte noch weniger spritzen als die Biobauern; weil Gaudi hier keine Kunst ist, sondern ein Zustand; weil Besucher hier herzlich willkommen sind – selbst die aus dem Norden; und weil die Tracht so gut passt wie der Lahm Philipp.

Freilich schauen auch viele Bayern skeptisch und ernst drein. Aus Heimatverdruss? Schmarrn! Es ist bloß der landestypische Grant, diese mürrisch-störrische Seligkeit, die die Zufriedenheit der Bayern nach außen verschleiert – und dazu ihre Gelassenheit und ihren Witz, ihre Offenheit und ihren Charme.

Wer dieses rätselhafte Volk nun kennenlernen will – oder wer Einheimischer ist und sich endlich selbst verstehen möchte – muss es intensiv studieren. **„Total alles über Bayern"** soll genau dabei helfen. Und weil die Bayern nicht nur für den Grant, sondern auch für ihre Maulfaulheit berüchtigt sind, kommt dieses Buch mit wenig Worten aus: Die gesammelten **Fakten**, **Zahlen**, **Weisheiten** sind in Infographiken und Illustrationen übersetzt.
Pack ma's.

Grüß Gott!

The Bavarian people can be truly hard to understand sometimes, and not just because of their dialects. Their faces are also difficult to read. Some Bavarians go through life with a smile on their face – maybe because in their home state FCB rhymes with BMW, because the police officers here shoot less often than the hunters, because the doctors give even fewer shots than the organic farmers, because fun here is not an art but a state of mind, because visitors are warmly welcomed – even those from up north, and because people get the same kick out of dressing up in folk costume as they do out of Philipp Lahm.

Or course, many Bavarians also have an air of scepticism and earnestness about them. Out of disappointment in their homeland perhaps? Nonsense! It's just the typical Bavarian grumpiness, a stubbornly cantankerous brand of serenity meant to hide their secret self-satisfaction from the outside world – along with their equanimity and wit, their openness and charm.

If you're now curious to meet these enigmatic folks – or if you're a native who would like to finally gain greater self-understanding — **"The Complete Bavaria"** is the perfect place to start. And because Bavarians are notorious for being not only ornery but also taciturn, this book makes do with few words. The collected **facts**, **figures** and **wisdom** are vividly conveyed by means of colourful infographics and illustrations.
Here we go...

Die Autoren / The authors
Die Gestalterinnen / The graphic designers

Du blau? Ich weiß!
It's all here in blue and white!

Die berühmten Farben bayerischer Institutionen, in einheitliche Formen gegossen / The famous colours of the Bavarian institutions, cast from a single mould.

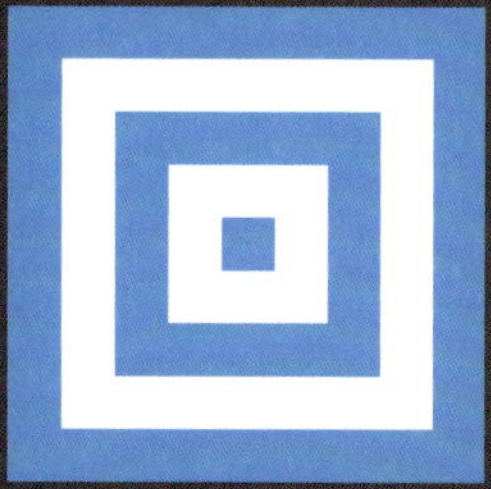

Landesfarben
State colours

CSU
(Christlich-Soziale Union in Bayern)
CSU (Christian Social Union in Bavaria)

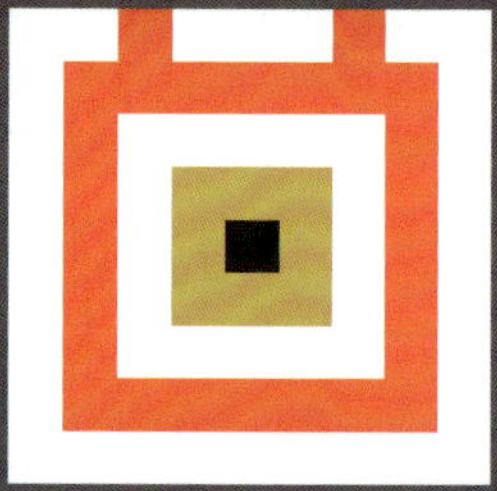

Wappen von München
Coat of arms of Munich

Bayerische Staatliche Polizei
Bavarian State Police

Bayerisches Wappen
Coat of arms of Bavaria

Münchner U-Bahn-Netz
Munich underground network

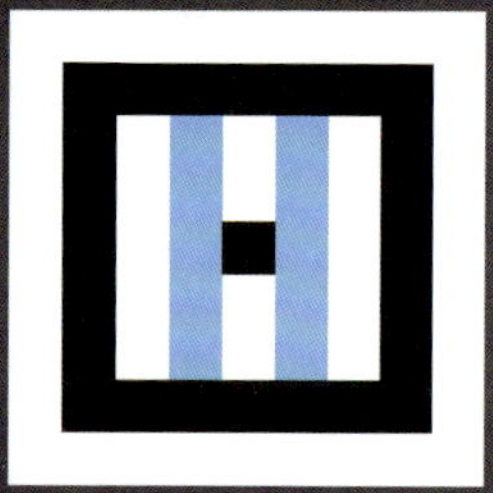

TSV 1860 München

FC Bayern München

Jupp „Osram" Heynckes,
ehemaliger Trainer des FC Bayern Münche
former FC Bayern München coach

ADAC

BMW

Audi

Siemens

Jim Knopf
(Augsburger Puppenkiste)
(Augsburger puppet show)

Neubau Lenbachhaus
New building for Lenbachhaus Museum

Augustiner-Bräu, Etikett
Augustiner Beer, label

Weißwurst mit süßem Senf
White sausages with sweet mustard

Leberkäse
Meat loaf

LaBrassBanda
Album „Europa“

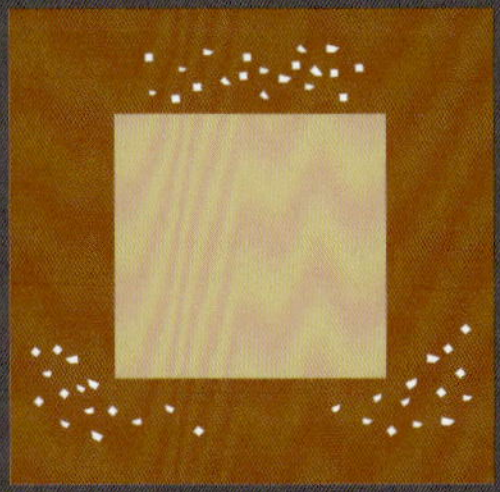

Brezn
Pretzel

Nürnberger
Rostbratwürste „Drei im Weggla“
Nuremberg roast bratwurst “Three on a roll“

Die Welt zu Gast bei Freunden
A time to make friends

Na, servus: Wo Bayerns Ausländer herkommen – und wo bayerische Auswanderer hingehen /
Na, servus: Where foreigners in Bavaria come from – and where Bavarian emigrants relocate

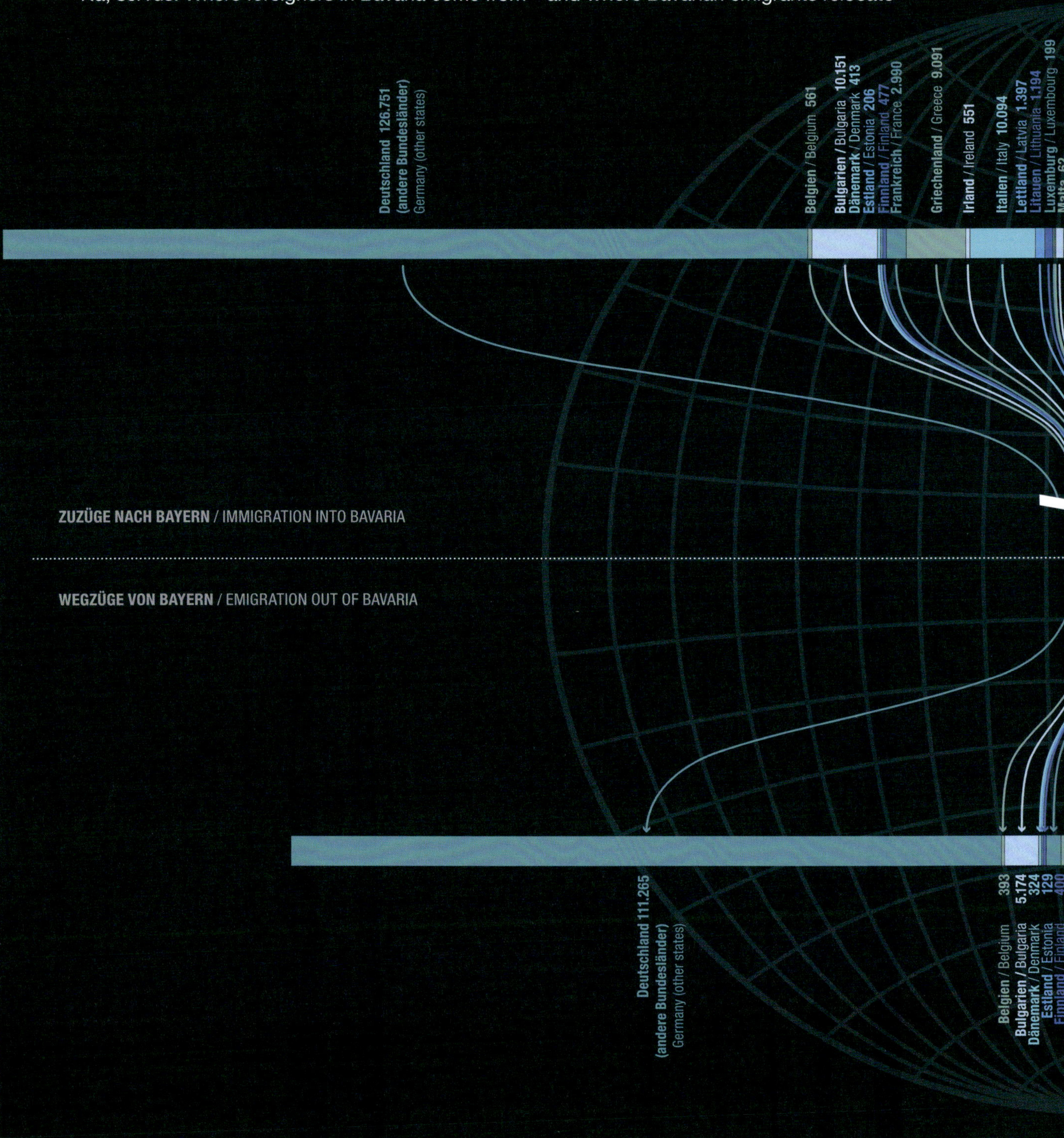

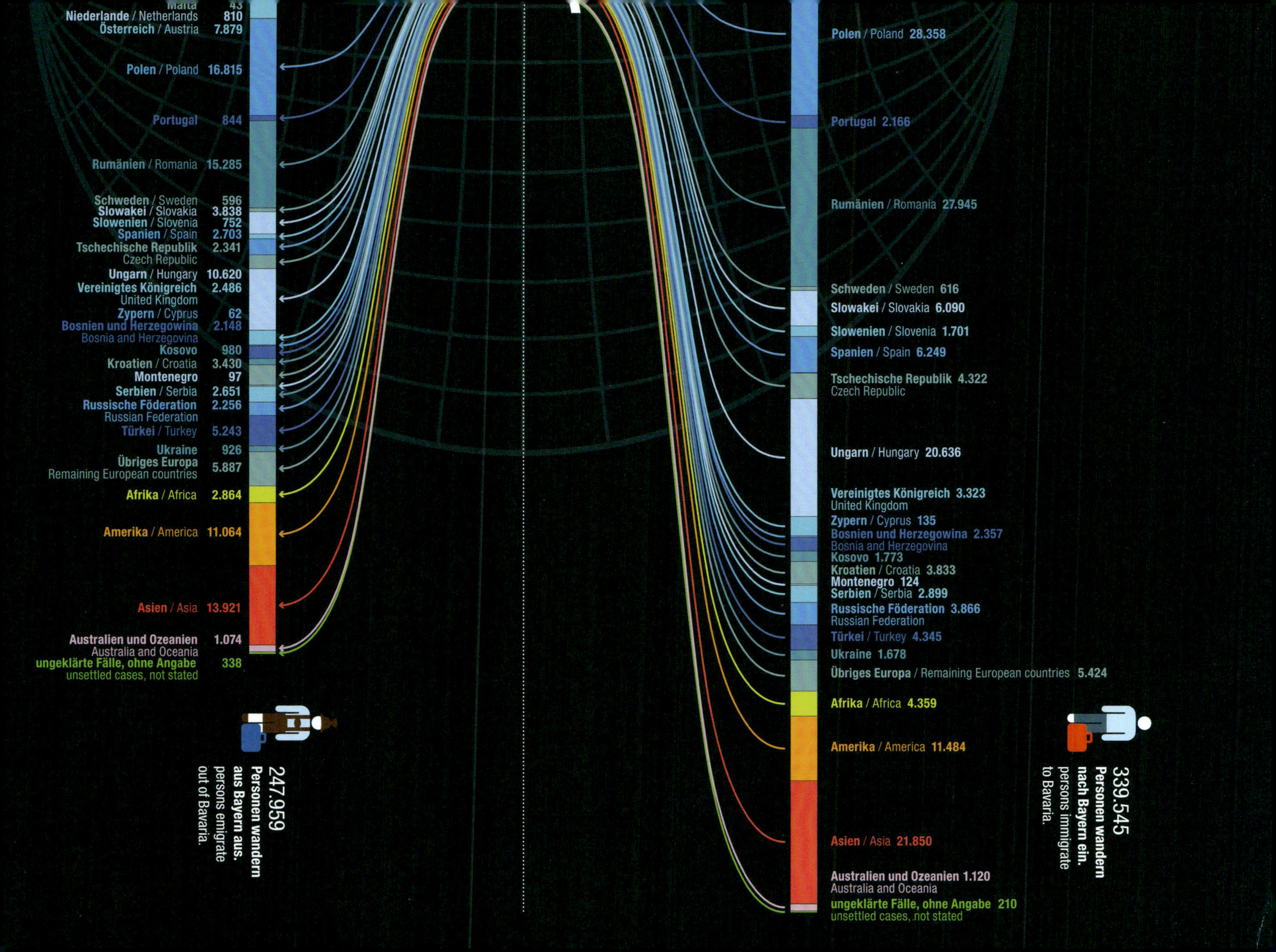
Malta 43
Niederlande / Netherlands 810
Österreich / Austria 7.879
Polen / Poland 16.815
Portugal 844
Rumänien / Romania 15.285
Schweden / Sweden 596
Slowakei / Slovakia 3.838
Slowenien / Slovenia 752
Spanien / Spain 2.703
Tschechische Republik 2.341
Czech Republic
Ungarn / Hungary 10.620
Vereinigtes Königreich 2.486
United Kingdom
Zypern / Cyprus 62
Bosnien und Herzegowina 2.148
Bosnia and Herzegovina
Kosovo 980
Kroatien / Croatia 3.430
Montenegro 97
Serbien / Serbia 2.651
Russische Föderation 2.256
Russian Federation
Türkei / Turkey 5.243
Ukraine 926
Übriges Europa 5.887
Remaining European countries
Afrika / Africa 2.864
Amerika / America 11.064
Asien / Asia 13.921
Australien und Ozeanien 1.074
Australia and Oceania
ungeklärte Fälle, ohne Angabe 338
unsettled cases, not stated
247.959
Personen wandern aus Bayern aus.
persons emigrate out of Bavaria.
Polen / Poland 28.358
Portugal 2.166
Rumänien / Romania 27.945
Schweden / Sweden 616
Slowakei / Slovakia 6.090
Slowenien / Slovenia 1.701
Spanien / Spain 6.249
Tschechische Republik 4.322
Czech Republic
Ungarn / Hungary 20.636
Vereinigtes Königreich 3.323
United Kingdom
Zypern / Cyprus 135
Bosnien und Herzegowina 2.357
Bosnia and Herzegovina
Kosovo 1.773
Kroatien / Croatia 3.833
Montenegro 124
Serbien / Serbia 2.899
Russische Föderation 3.866
Russian Federation
Türkei / Turkey 4.345
Ukraine 1.678
Übriges Europa / Remaining European countries 5.424
Afrika / Africa 4.359
Amerika / America 11.484
Asien / Asia 21.850
Australien und Ozeanien 1.120
Australia and Oceania
ungeklärte Fälle, ohne Angabe 210
unsettled cases, not stated
339.545
Personen wandern nach Bayern ein.
persons immigrate to Bavaria.

Mia san mia

We are what we are

Die beliebtesten Vornamen und gängigsten Nachnamen der Bayern / Bavaria's most popular first names and most common surnames

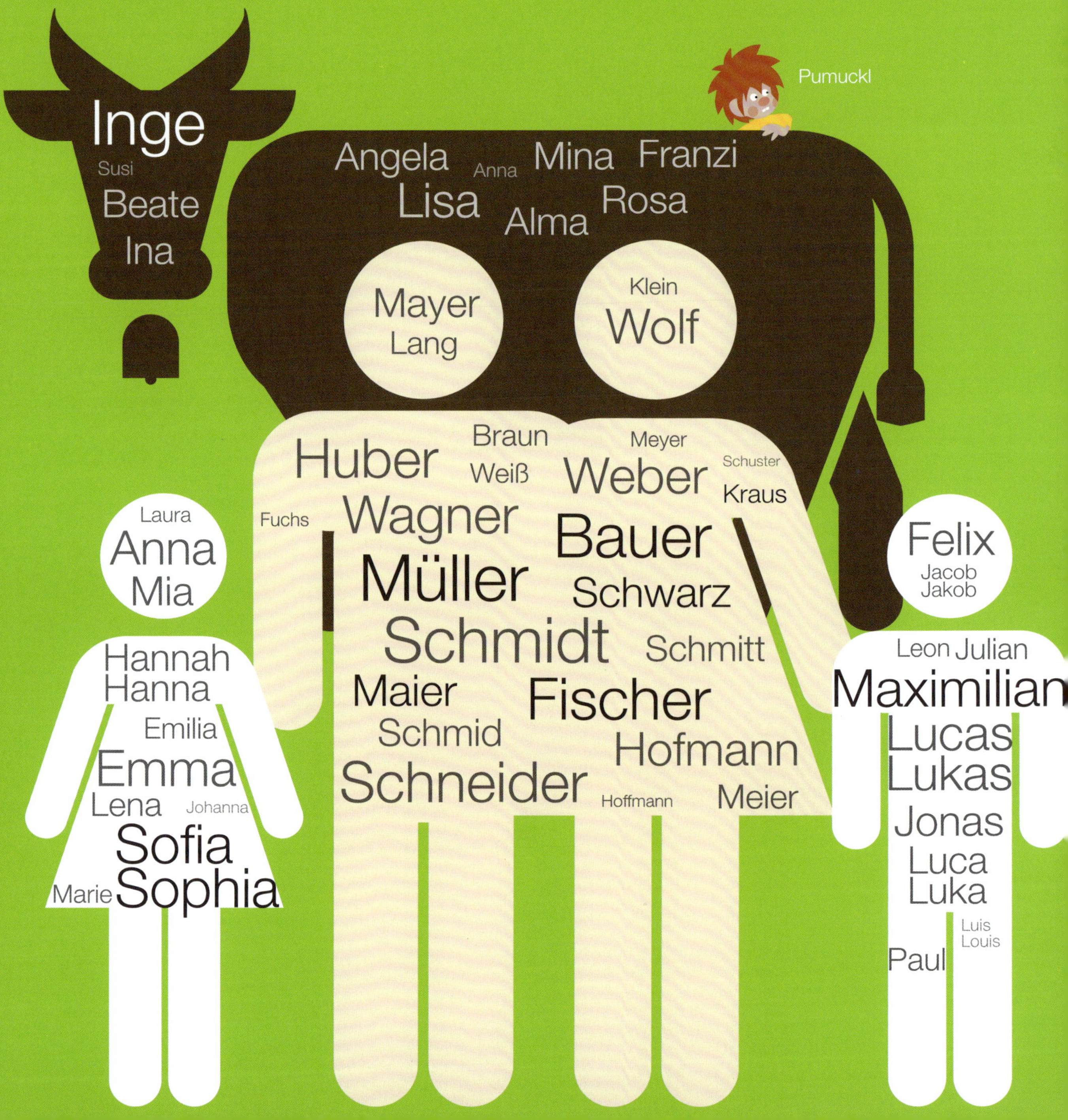

Die geografische Verbreitung der typischen Familiennamen Bayerns

The geographical distribution of typical Bavarian family names

Insel der Narrischen
Island of fools

Ja, wo samma denn? Wer denkt sich solche Ortsnamen aus? Und das in Bayern. Und außerhalb sowieso. / What kind of place is this anyway? Who thinks up town names like these? And in Bavaria of all places. Just like everywhere else in the world.

Das Internationale Samba-Festival in Coburg lockt jährlich rund 200.000 Besucher an und ist damit das größte Samba-Festival außerhalb Brasiliens. / The International Samba Festival in Coburg lures some 200,000 visitors and is thus the biggest samba festival outside Brazil.
Tschechischer Ozean / Czech Ocean
Alpenriff / Alpine Reef
Strahlungen
Hölle
Oberkotzau
Poppenhausen
Busendorf
Prügel
Krötennest
Kümmel
Wampen
Kotzendorf
Kamerun
Strullendorf
rankfurt
Prügeldorf
Ochsenschenkel
Wichsenstein
Lachheim
Thomasgschieß
Mailheim
Ursulapoppenricht
Sack
Poppenreuth
Sandberg
Kotzheim
Muschenried
Leichendorf
Drahtzieher
Feucht
Gschieß
Holland
Ameisenbrücke
Aha
Geilsheim
Titting
Möhren
Geländer
Fischbehälter
Vogelsang
Speckbrodi
Seppenhausen
Bierhütte
Oberanschiessing
Branntweinhäuser
Unsernherrn
Frommerding
Prag
Schmatzhausen
Naßkamping
Brennschinken
Glucking
Heimlichleiden
Mießling
Göttersdorf
Ort
Pumpernudl
Schlucking
Witzling
Hascherkeller
Wunder
Motzenhofen
Gammelsdorf
Pfannenstiel
Frauentödling
Blasen
Paradies
Klobach
Streitheim
Schmarnzell
Narrenstetten
Roßtauschen
Luderbach
Heimat
Schlipps
Troll
Großmaulberg
Schlupfing
Bieselbach
Kleinviecht
Afterhausen
Tittenkofen
Ellenbogen
Faulkäs
Witzighausen
Kissing
Sixtnitgern
Ewigkeit
Gaymoos
Rattenkirchen
Schlapping
Howaschen
Galgen
Niedergottsau
Poing
Dreifaltigkeit
Schrottfurt
Höllhund
Tussenhausen
Froschkern
Unnütz
Rausch
Elend
Glatzenberg
Katzenhirn
Unterhöslwang
Lachen
Baiern
Öd
Seppl im Holz
Frühling
Pups
Petting
Tuntenhausen
Antwort
Fraßhausen
Wimmern
Ampo
Zacking
Grabenstätt
Übersee
Albern
Heiland
Bürstenstiel
Miesbach
Wien
Bibelöd
Kloo
Bethlehem
Ostern
Köln
Mauslochsteig
N
W
O
S

Otto Normalbayer
Just your average Bavarian

Was zeichnet einen durchschnittlichen Bayern aus? / What makes a Bavarian?

20,81 € | 17,63 €
Bruttolohn pro Stunde
Gross wage per hour

1.033 € | 535 €
Monatliche Rente
Monthly pension

17,6 | 18,2
Alter, wenn die Bayern mit dem Rauchen beginnen
The age Bavarians start smoking

28,2 % | 19 %
rauchen
smoke

45,1 m²
Wohnfläche
Size of living space

511 kg
Abfall pro Jahr
Waste per year

1,78 m | 1,65 m
Körpergröße
Height

26,3 kg/m² | 24,6 kg/m²
Body-Mass-Index (BMI)
Body Mass Index (BMI)

82,9 kg | 67,1 kg
Gewicht
Weight

FETTE ZUSATZINFO
WEIGHTY FACT

84,3 kg | 80,3 kg
Verheiratete Bayern sind 4 kg schwerer als ledige.
Married Bavarian men are 4 kg heavier than singles.

68,1 kg | 63,4 kg
Verheiratete Bayerinnen sind 4,7 kg schwerer als ledige.
Married Bavarian women are 4.7 kg heavier than singles.

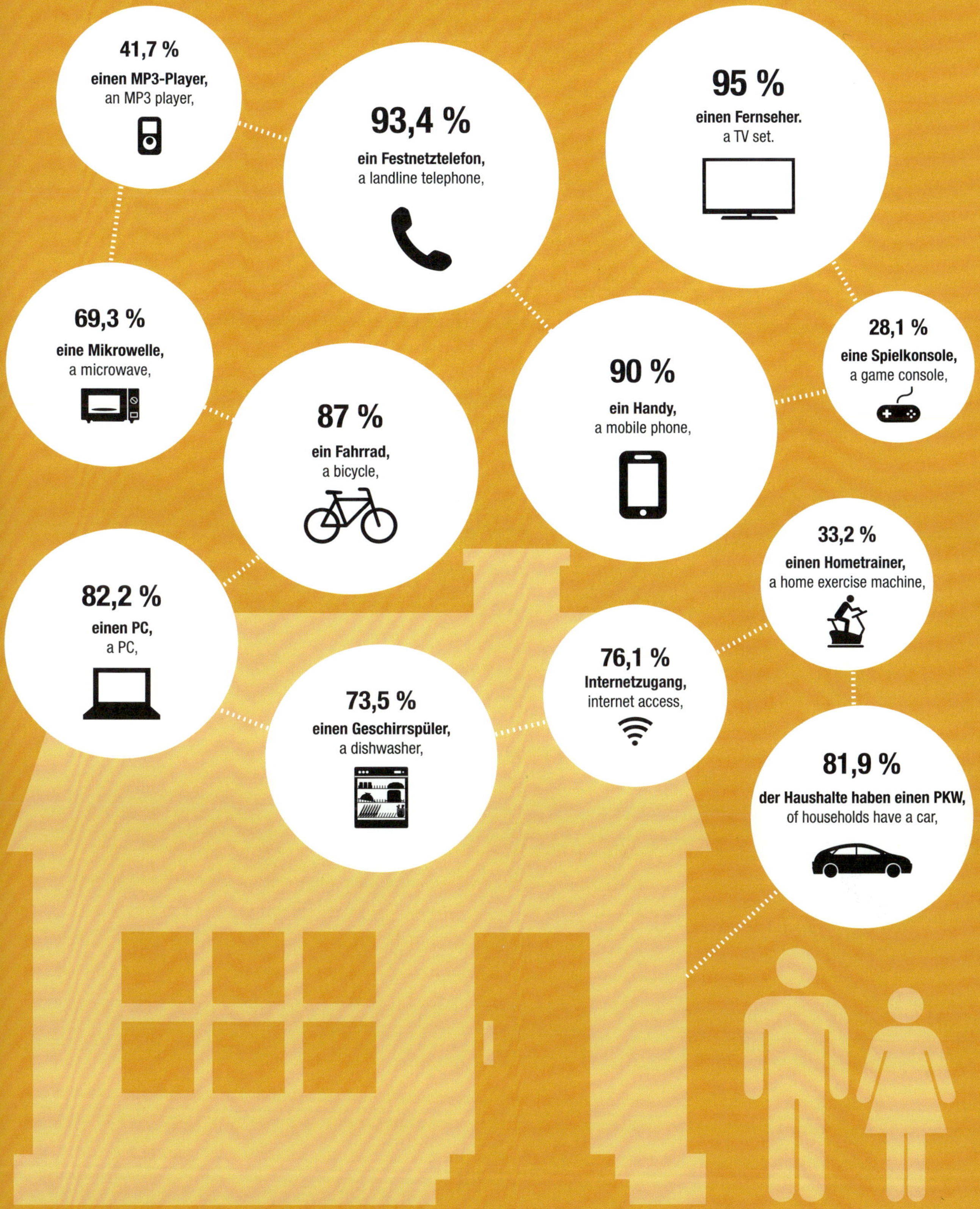

TYPISCHE BAYERISCHE HAUSHALTE (UMFASSEN 2,06 BAYERN)
TYPICAL BAVARIAN HOUSEHOLDS (COMPRISE 2.06 BAVARIANS)

Was machen die bloß?
What on earth do they do?

Heilende Hände, schlimme Finger, grüne Daumen – die Berufe und Berufungen der Bayern. Eine qualifizierte Auswahl. / Healing hands, sneaky fingers, green thumbs – the occupations and vocations of the Bavarians. A qualified selection.

6.606.000
Erwerbstätige
employed

248.840
Arbeitslose
unemployed

24.935
selbstständige Ärzte (in freier Praxis)
self-employed physicians (in private practice)

1.092
Kinderärzte
paediatricians

923
Augenärzte
ophthalmologists

10.783
Zahnärzte (in freier Praxis)
dentists (in private practice)

24.646
Krankenhausärzte
hospital physicians

64.412
Krankenpflegepersonal im Krankenhaus
hospital nursing staff

94.501
Mitarbeiter in Pflegeheimen
nursing home staff

13.716
Apotheker
dispensing chemists

1
Boandlkramer
Grim Reaper

357
Bestatter
undertakers

1.500.216
Schüler
pupils

14.489
Waldorfschüler
Waldorf school pupils

332.229
Studierende
university students

92.244
Lehrer
teachers

257.400
Arbeitskräfte in der Landwirtschaft
agricultural workers

38.400
Saisonarbeitskräfte in der Landwirtschaft
seasonal agricultural workers

467
Menschlein tummeln sich im Wimmelbuch München
little people are concealed in the Munich hidden object book.

23
Fußball-WM-Teilnehmer (2014) aus bayerischen Vereinen
World Cup football participants (2014) from Bavarian clubs

121.876
Straftäter
criminal offenders

9.469
Knackis
convicts

44
Mörder
murderers

4
Tatort-Hauptkommissare
chief inspectors on the TV series "Tatort"

1.069
Räuber und Erpresser
robbers and extortionists

18.684
Diebe
thieves

115
Geldfälscher
counterfeiters

4.498
Urkundenfälscher
document forgers

31.929
Straßenverkehrssünder
traffic offenders

1.282
Straßenbahnführer
tram drivers

16.622
Busfahrer
bus drivers

301
Lokführer
train drivers

1
Drei-Sterne-Koch
three-star chef

46.000
Jäger
hunters

4.680
katholische Priester
Catholic priests

4.063
evangelische Pfarrer
Protestant pastors
davon weiblich
thereof female
1.039

Bayerische Gebärden
Bavarian signs

Wie Gehörlose bayerische Begriffe gebärden – und warum die im Süden manchmal anders aussehen als im Norden / How the deaf sign typical Bavarian terms – and why they sometimes look different in the south than in the north

BREZN / PRETZEL

SONNTAG / SUNDAY

Im Süden ist der Sonntag mit einem Kirchgang verbunden, im Norden mit feiner Kleidung.
In the south, Sunday is associated with going to church and in the north, with dressing up.

WEISSWURST
WHITE SAUSAGE

In Bayern haben sich die Metzger früher die Wurstketten über die Schulter geworfen.
The Bavarian butchers used to throw the sausage links over their shoulder.

RETTICH / RADISH

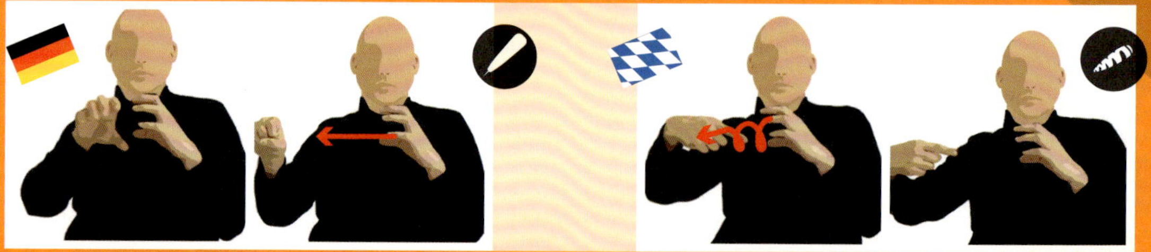

Im Norden wird die Form eines Rettichs gebärdet, in Bayern das Aufschneiden des Radis.
People in the north sign the form of a radish and those in Bavaria sign cutting a radish.

SCHWEINSHAXN / PORK KNUCKLES

SCHWEINEBRATEN / SCHWEINEBRATEN

MÜNCHEN / MUNICH

Ein Krone für den Ur-Münchner Ludwig I.
A crown, standing for Munich's famous son, Ludwig I

ZUGSPITZE

Der Berg mit dem eigenartigen Gipfel
The mountain with the strangely shaped peak

THEO WAIGEL

Der CSU-Mann mit den Schnauzern über den Augen
The Christian Social Union party member with the moustaches over his eyes

EDMUND STOIBER

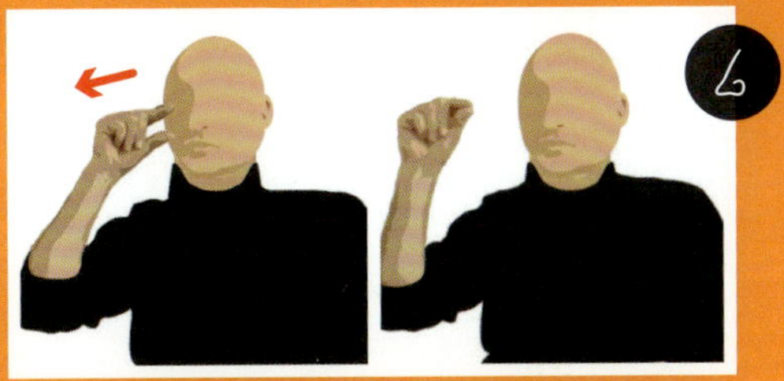

Der CSU-Mann mit der spitzen Nase
The Christian Social Union party member with the pointy nose

DIRNDLKLEID / DIRNDL DRESS

LEDERHOSE

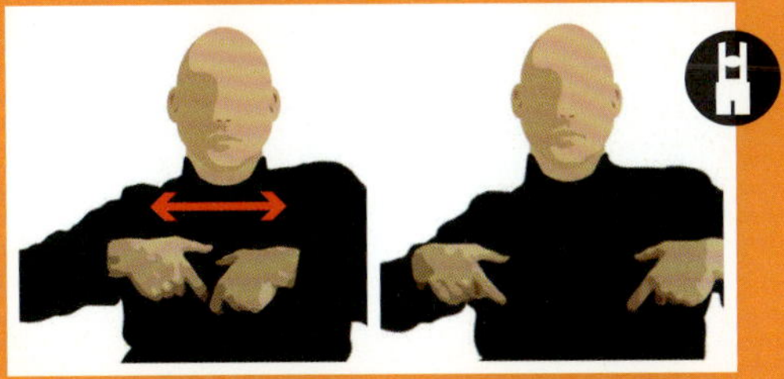

BAYERN / BAVARIA

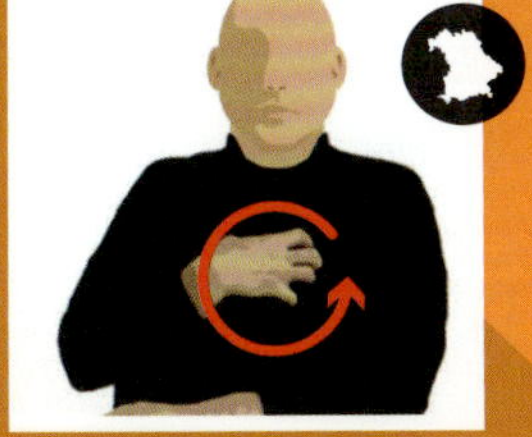

Die Gebärde für den Löwen steht auch für Bayern.
The sign for lion also stands for Bavaria.

OBERBAYERN UND NIEDERBAYERN
UPPER BAVARIA AND LOWER BAVARIA

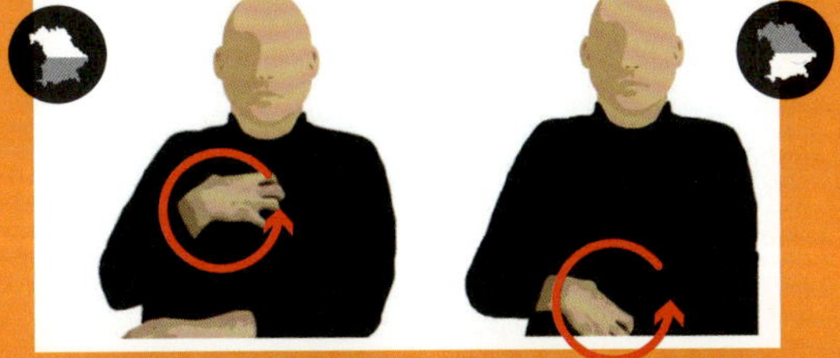

Zum Schluss noch ein dreckiger Witz unter Gehörlosen: die (natürlich falschen) Gebärden für Ober- und Niederbayern
Finally, a little dirty joke amongst the deaf: the (incorrect, of course) signs for Upper and Lower Bavaria

Ja, was glauben sie denn?
You gotta have faith

Die Bayern sind für ihre Frömmigkeit bekannt – sie sind so katholisch, dass sogar die Kurve der Kirchenaustritte aussieht wie ein Gotteshaus. / The Bavarians are renowned for their piousness – they're so Catholic that even the curve mapping those leaving the church looks like a house of God.

Der Papst / The Pope

Benedikt XVI.

*** 1927 in Marktl als** / as
Joseph Aloisius Ratzinger

2012
1. Twitter-Meldung:
„Liebe Freunde! Gerne verbinde ich mich mit euch über Twitter. Danke für die netten Antworten. Von Herzen segne ich euch."
1st tweet:
"Dear friends! I am pleased to get in touch with you through Twitter. Thank you for your generous response. I bless all of you from my heart."

19.04.2005
Wahl zum ersten deutschen Papst seit 1523
Elected as the first German pope since 1523.

28.02.2013
Amtsverzicht / Resignation

188.936,88 €
erzielte 2005 sein früheres Auto, ein VW Golf 2005, bei einer Versteigerung auf eBay.
Price paid for his former car, a VW Golf 2005, on eBay.

Durchschnittsalter bei der Eheschließung
Average marriage age

	Mann	Frau
1970	28,2	24,7
1990	30,3	27,3
2012	37,1	33,9

Unehelich geboren Kinder
Children born out of wedlock

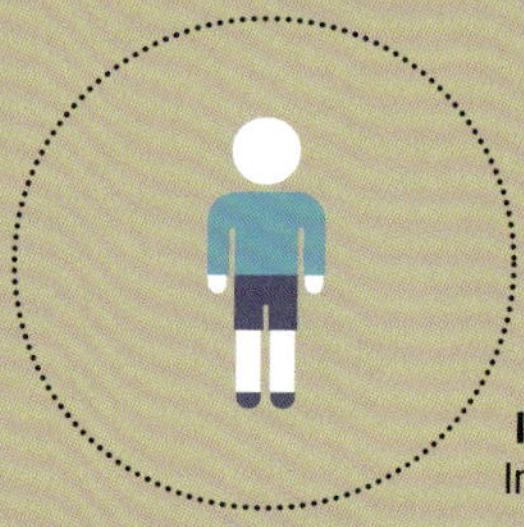

1970
7 %

2011
26 %

In Restdeutschland
In the rest of Germany
35 %

Konfessionen / Confessions

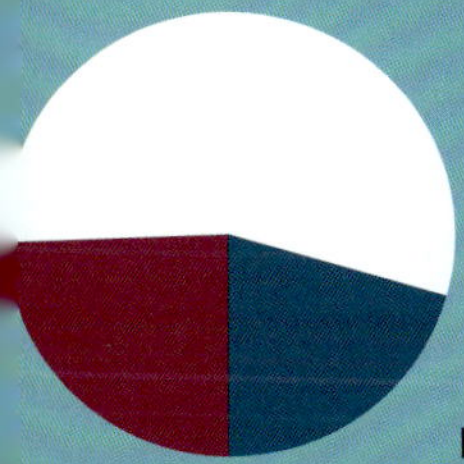

Römisch-katholisch
Roman Catholic
54,8 %

Evangelisch
Protestant
20,7 %

Andere
Other
24,5 %

Altötting

Wallfahrtsort seit mehr als 1250 Jahren
Pilgrimage site for more than 1,250 years

Ziel: „Die schwarze Madonna“
Destination: “The Black Madonna”

Mehr als 1 Million Pilger und Besucher pro Jahr
More than 1 mil. pilgrims and visitors per year

Die zwei meistdiskutierten Bücher im Ort
The two most-discussed books in town

1. Die Bibel / The Bible

2. Das Scheißleben meines Vaters, das Scheißleben meiner Mutter und meine eigene Scheißjugend
My father's shitty life, my mother's shitty life, and my own shitty youth
2011, von / by **Andreas Altmann, aufgewachsen im Ort**
who grew up in the town

Austritte aus den bayerischen Bistümern und aus der Evangelisch-Lutherischen Kirche in Bayern

People leaving the Bavarian bishoprics and the Protestant Church in Bavaria

Missbrauch in katholischen Einrichtungen wird aufgedeckt
Child abuse in Catholic institutions is exposed.

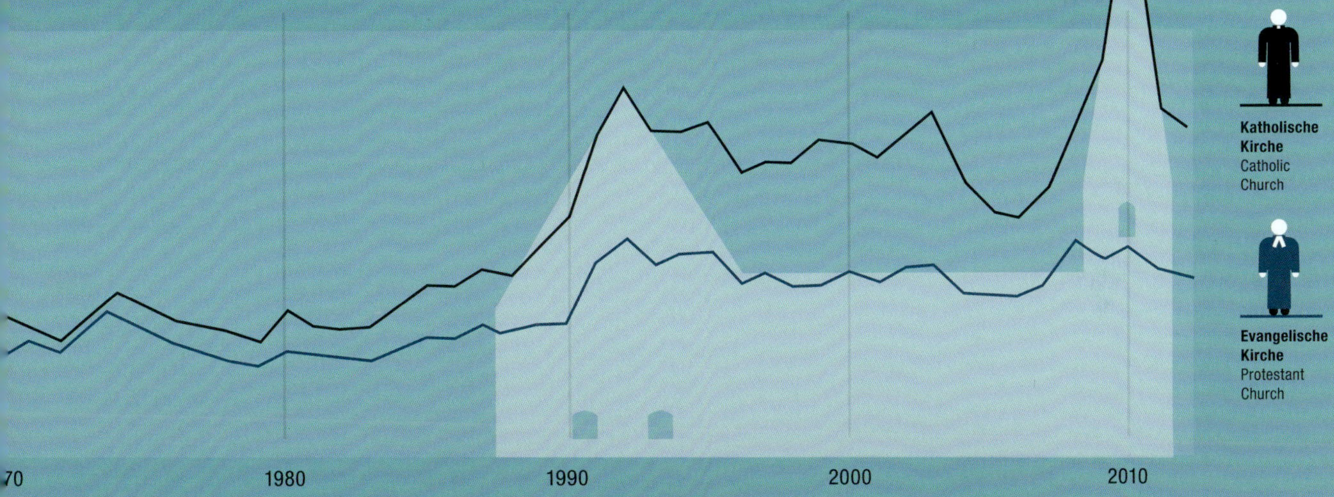

Kapelle St. Maria (Altötting)
Shrine of Our Lady of Altötting

Was lange währt …

Good things come …

Scheidungen im Jahr 2013
Divorces in 2013
24.797

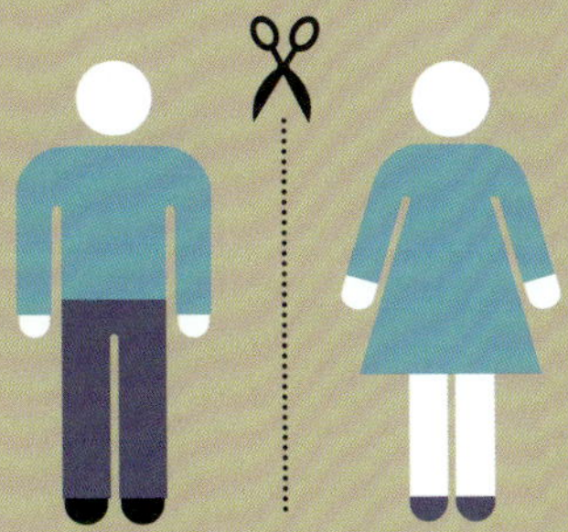

davon bei Ehedauer unter 1 Jahr
thereof marriages lasting less than 1 year
7
sicherste Phase
safest phase

davon bei Ehedauer von mehr als 25 Jahren
thereof marriages lasting more than 25 years
3.791
unsicherste Phase
unsafest phase

Wo was los ist
The lay of the land

Wie die Fläche Bayerns genutzt wird – eine flurbereinigte Graphik /
How Bavaria's land is used – a graphic plot

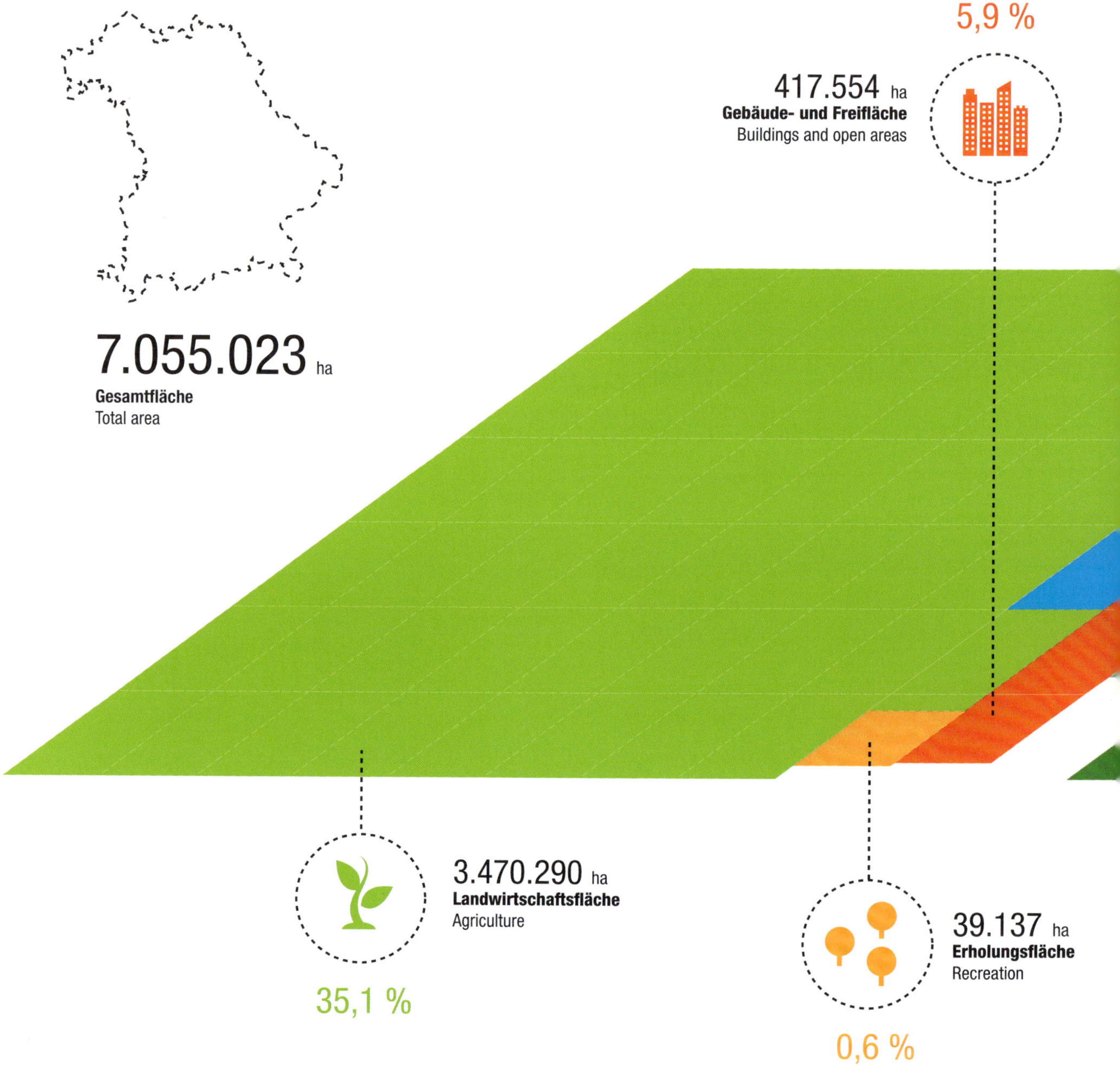

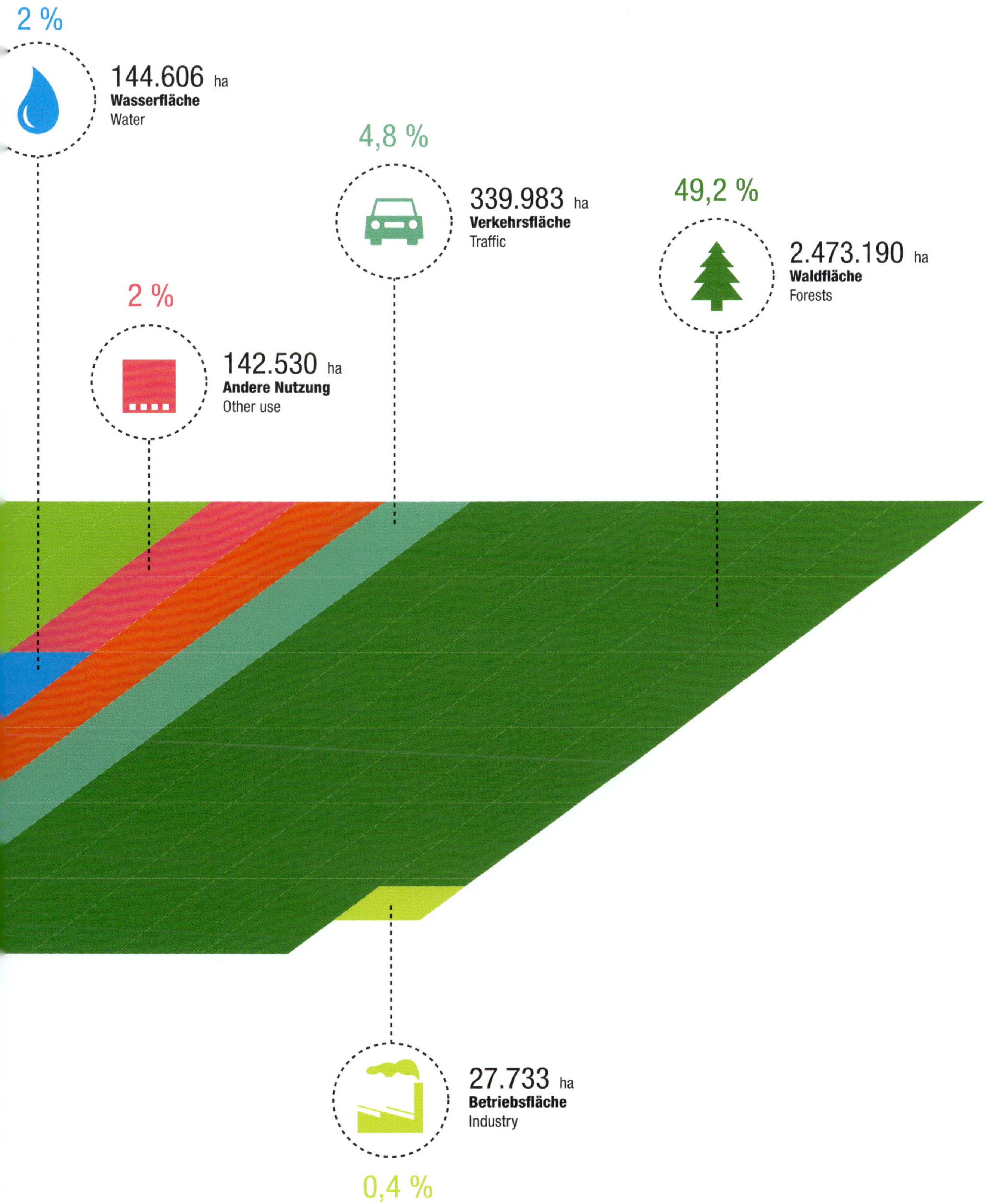
2 %
144.606 ha
Wasserfläche
Water
4,8 %
339.983 ha
Verkehrsfläche
Traffic
49,2 %
2.473.190 ha
Waldfläche
Forests
2 %
142.530 ha
Andere Nutzung
Other use
27.733 ha
Betriebsfläche
Industry
0,4 %

Ganz oben, ganz unten
At the top, at the bottom

Der Freistaat hat im föderalistischen Deutschland eine Ausnahmestellung – so oder so. /
In federalist Germany, Bavaria is an exception – for better or for worse.

BESSER ALS ALLE ANDEREN BUNDESLÄNDER
BETTER THAN ALL OTHER GERMAN STATES

Höchste Wirtschaftskraft
Most economic power

Beste Förderung des ökologischen Landbaus
Best promotion of organic farming

Beste Förderung der beruflichen Bildung
Best promotion of vocational education

12
Meiste Feiertage
+ vielerorts Mariä Himmelfahrt
+ Friedensfest in Augsburg
Most holidays
+ in many places the Feast of the Assumption
+ the Augsburg Peace Festival

Niedrigste Arbeitslosenqu
Lowest unemployment rate
3,5 %
(Juni / June, **2014)**

Bundesdurchschnitt
National average
6,5 %

Höchste Ausgaben für Wurst
Highest expenditures on sausage
372 €
(pro Magen und Jahr / per stomach and year)

Wenigste Straftaten
Fewest crimes
5.073
(je 100.000 Einwohner / per 100,000 inhabitants, **2013)**

Bundesdurchschnitt
National average
7.404

Höchstes verfügbares Nettoeinkommen
Highest disposable net income
1.631 €
(pro Bayer / per Bavarian**)**

Bundesdurchschnitt
National average
1.345 €

Größte Spendierhose beim Länderfinanzausgleich
Biggest contributors to the fiscal equalisation scheme
4.320.000.000 €
(2013)

Höchste Nachtclub-Dichte
Highest night club density
4,46
(je 100.000 Einwohner / per 100,000 inhabitants**)**

Und noch ein Fleißkärtchen für Starnberg: Ort mit höchster Ärzte-Dichte, den meisten Einkommensmillionären sowie der längsten Lebenserwartung
And a special gold star for Starnberg: the town with the highest density of physicians, the most self-made millionaires and the longest life expectancy

SCHLECHTER ALS DER REST DES LANDES
WORSE THAN IN THE REST OF THE COUNTRY

Höchste Selbstmordrate
Highest suicide rate
14,1
(je 100.000 Einwohner /
per 100,000 inhabitants, **2010)**
Bundesdurchschnitt
National average
12,3

Schlechteste Masern-Impfquote bei Kleinkindern
Worst red measles vaccination rate amongst small children
56,4 %

Höchste Sitzenbleiber-Quote bei Schülern (Klassen 5 bis 10)
Highest failure rate amongst pupils (grades 5 to 10)
4,6 %
(2011)

Stadt mit höchstem Kaufpreis für Eigentumswohnungen: München
City with the highest-priced condominiums: Munich
4.155 € / m²
(2013)

ieseste Beicht-Quote
er Fremdgeher
orest confession rate
nongst adulterers
ur / only
32 %
erichten dem Partner
om Seitensprung
ll their partner
out their affair

Niedrigste Durchschnittstemperatur
Lowest average temperature
9,5 °C
(im Frühling / in spring, **2014)**
Bundesdurchschnitt
National average
10,1° C

eiste Menschen
Gefängnis
lativ zur
völkerung)
ost prisoners
lative to
population)

chleppendster
usbau der
anztagesschulen
owest conversion to
l-day schools

Höchster Mangel an Altenpflegern
Highest shortage of elderly caregivers
24 %
aller unbesetzten Stellen in Deutschland entfallen auf den Freistaat.
of all vacant positions in Germany are in Bavaria.

Wenigste Frauenhaus-Plätze: Auf 18.765 Frauen kommt 1 Platz.
Fewest women's shelter places: There is only 1 place for every 18,765 women.

Meiste Drogentote
Most drug-related deaths
230
(2013)

Meiste Badetote
Most fatal swimming accidents
73
(2013)

Meiste Pilzvergiftungen
Most mushroom poisonings
43 %
aller bundesweit gemeldeten Patienten
of all patients registered nationwide

Die Summe der einzelnen Teile
The sum of the individual parts

Der Freistaat, unendliche Weiten: 2.031 kreisangehörige Gemeinden, 71 Landkreise, 25 kreisfreie Städte – und sieben ziemlich verschiedene Regierungsbezirke / The Free State of Bavaria in all its vastness: 2,031 district towns and municipalities, 71 counties, 25 independent cities – and seven quite diverse administrative districts

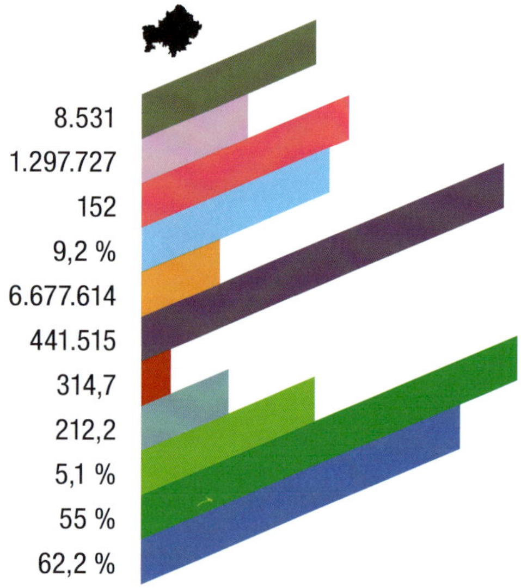

UNTERFRANKEN / LOWER FRANCONIA
Würzburg

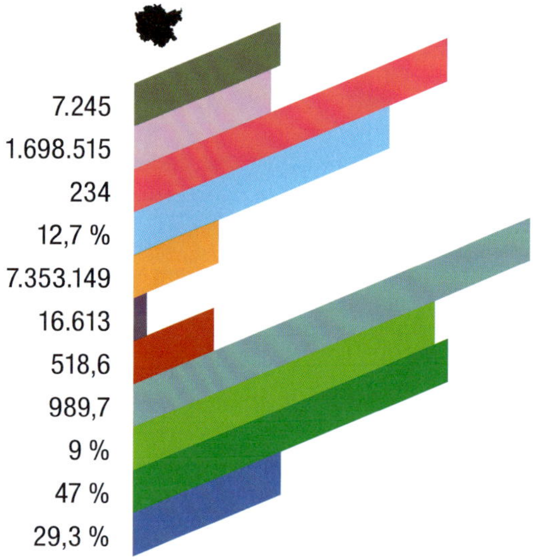

MITTELFRANKEN / MIDDLE FRANCONIA
Ansbach

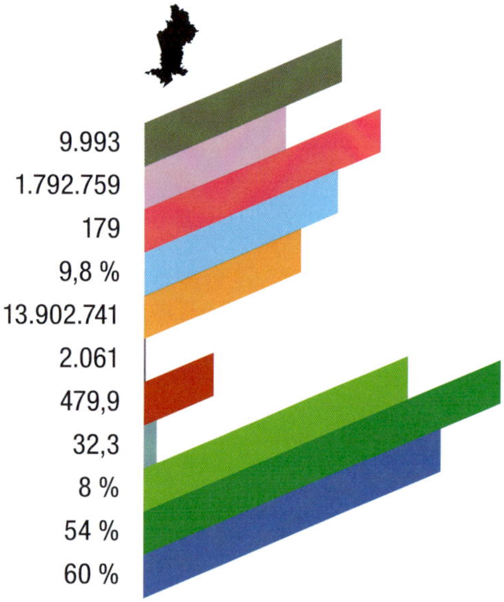

SCHWABEN / SWABIA
Augsburg

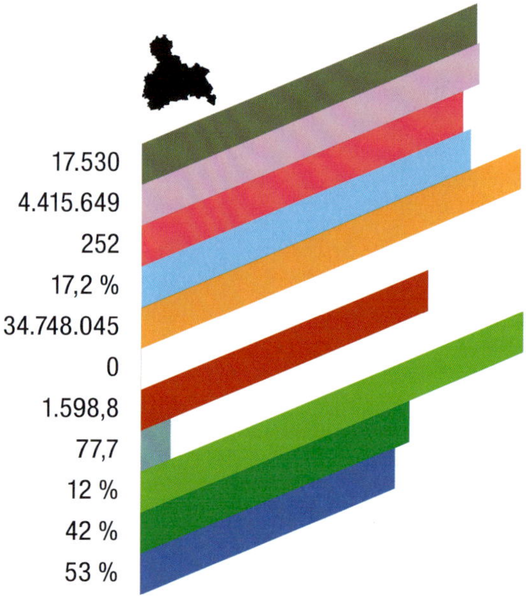

OBERBAYERN / UPPER BAVARIA
München / Munich

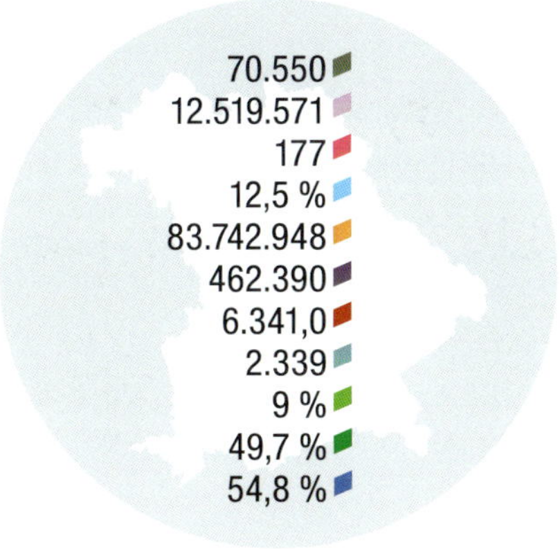

BAYERN / BAVARIA
München / Munich

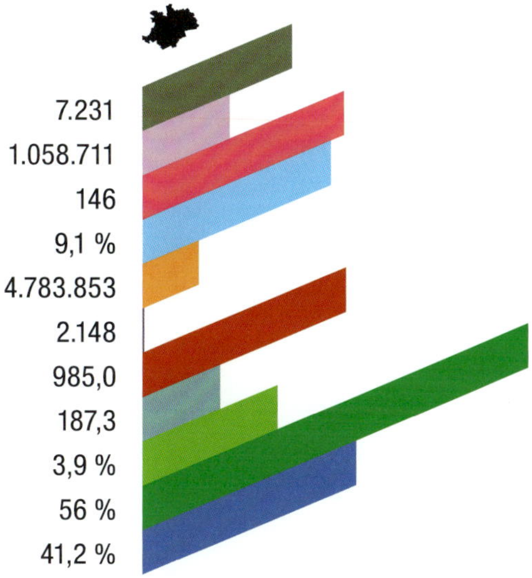

OBERFRANKEN / UPPER FRANCONIA
Bayreuth

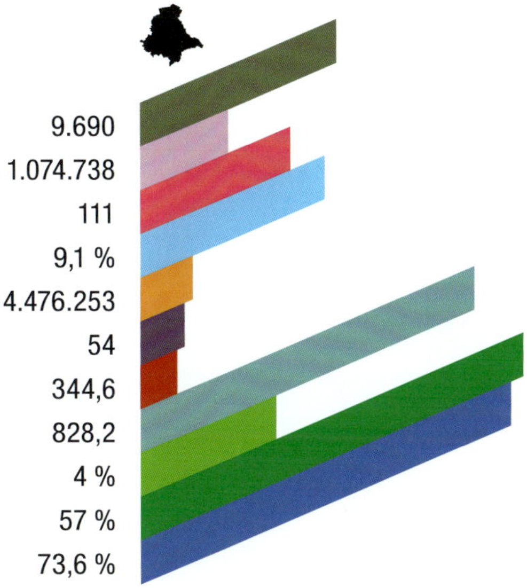

OBERPFALZ / UPPER PALATINATE
Regensburg

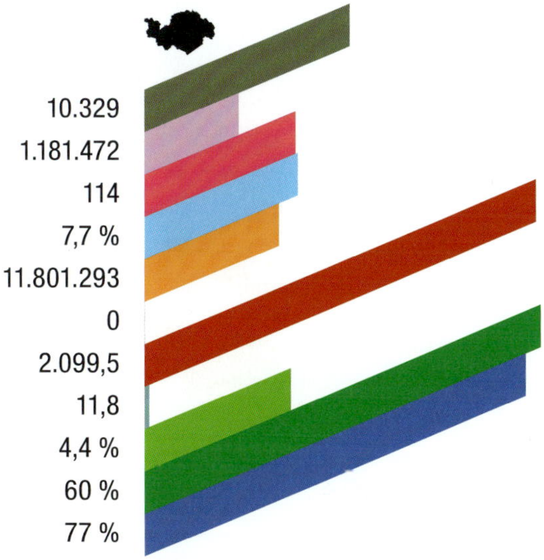

NIEDERBAYERN / LOWER BAVARIA
Landshut

- **Fläche** / Area (in km²)
- **Einwohner** / Total population
- **Einwohner** / Population (**je**/per km²)
- **Einwohner mit Hochschulabschluss** Residents with a university degree
- **Touristenübernachtungen** Overnight stays by tourists
- **Weinerzeugung** / Wine production (in hl)
- **Schlachtungen** / Livestock slaughtered (in 1.000 / 1,000s)
- **Speisefischerzeugung: Gemeiner Karpfen** Edible fish production: common carp (in t)
- **Ausländeranteil** / Ratio of foreigners
- **Wohneigentumsquote** Home-ownership rate
- **Katholiken** / Catholics

Regierungssitz / Seat of government

540–550

Einwanderung der Bajuwaren in das Land zwischen Donau und Alp[en]
The Bajuwars migrate to the land between Danube and Alps.

555

Erster Beleg eines bairischen Herzogtums mit Sitz in Freising unter den Agilolfingern
First documentation of a Bavarian duchy with seat in Freising under the Agilolfings

788

Ende des älteren Stammesherzogtums
End of the older feudal duchy

957–976

Abtrennung des Herzogtums Kärnten: Ausdehnung Baierns bis an die Adria
Secession of the Duchy of Carinthia: Bavaria expands to the Adriatic Coast.

1002

Wahl des bayerischen Herzogs Heinrich zum deutschen König
Bavarian Duke Heinrich elected German King

1070–1180

Regentschaft der Welfen (mit Unterbrechungen)
Rule of the Guelfs (with interruptions)

1180

Ende des jüngeren Stammesherzogtums
End of the younger feudal duchy

1180–1918

Regentschaft der Wittelsbacher
Rule of the Wittelsbachs

1830

Otto I. wird König von Griechenland.
Otto I becomes King of Greece.

1866

Niederlage gegen die Preußen im Deutschen Krieg
Bavaria is defeated by Prussia in the Prussian-German War.

1871

Bayern wird Teil des neu gegründeten Deutschen Reichs.
Bavaria becomes part of the newly established German Reich.

1918

Ende der Monarchie: Bayern wird „Freistaat“, also republikanisch
End of the monarchy: Bavaria becomes a "Free State", i.e. republican.

1919

Niederschlagung der kommunistischen Räterepublik durch Freikorps
Bavarian Communist Republic is defeated by the "Free Corps".

1923

Hitlerputsch in München, der späteren „Hauptstadt der Bewegung“
Hitler putsch in Munich, later the "Capital of the Movement"

1934

Gleichschaltung Bayerns mit dem Reich durch die Nazis
Bavaria is "brought into line" with the Reich by the Nazis.

1943

Verurteilung der Mitglieder der Widerstandsgruppe „Weiße Rose“
Conviction of the member[s] of the resistance group "White Rose"

Es war einmal ... der Bajuware

Once upon a time ... the Bajuwars

Die lange Geschichte Bayerns in 27 Sauseschritten / The long history of Bavaria in 27 quicksteps

1255

Erste Landesteilung in
)ber- und Niederbayern
First partition into Upper
and Lower Bavaria

1314

Ludwig der Bayer als erster Wittelsbacher auf dem Kaiserthron
Ludwig the Bavarian is first Wittelsbach on the imperial throne.

1506

Wiedervereinigung des Herzogtums nach dem Landshuter Erbfolgekrieg – Primogeniturordnung
Reunification of the duchy after the Landshut War of Succession – primogeniture instituted

1549

Berufung von Jesuiten an die Landesuniversität Ingolstadt – Gegenreformation
Jesuits appointed to key positions at the State University of Ingolstadt – Counter-Reformation

1623

Erhebung zum Kurfürstentum
Bavaria elevated to the status of electorate

1777

Vereinigung von Bayern und Kurpfalz
Unification of Bavaria and Electoral Palatinate

1806

Erhebung zum Königreich und Gewinn fränkischer, schwäbischer und österreichischer Gebiete
Bavaria is elevated to status of kingdom and acquires Franconian, Swabian and Austrian territories.

1825

Unter Ludwig I. Umbenennung Baierns in Bayern
Under Ludwig I, "Baiern" is renamed "Bayern".

1946

Volksentscheid über
die bayerische
/erfassung, Verlust der
npfalz, Wahl von Hans Ehard
J) zum Ministerpräsidenten
eferendum on the Bavarian
Constitution, loss of the
ineland-Palatinate, election
of Hans Ehard (CSU)
as Minister-President

1949

Bayern wird als Bundesland Teil der Bundesrepublik Deutschland
Bavaria becomes a federal state in the Federal Republic of Germany.

1957

Wahl von Hanns Seidel (CSU) zum Ministerpräsidenten, nach seinem Rücktritt wieder Ehard
Hanns Seidel (CSU) is elected Minister-President, and after his resignation Ehard again.

Das CSUniversum
The CSUniverse

Die CSU, die kleine große Schwesterpartei der CDU, tritt ausschließlich im Freistaat an – traditionell mit überwältigendem Erfolg. Die Farbe der Partei ist schwarz. Andere Farben sind im politischen Bayern kaum bekannt. / The CSU (Christian Social Union), the big little-sister party of the CDU (Christian Democratic Union), only stands for election in the Free State of Bavaria – traditionally with resounding success. The party colour is black. Other colours hardly appear at all on the state's political landscape.

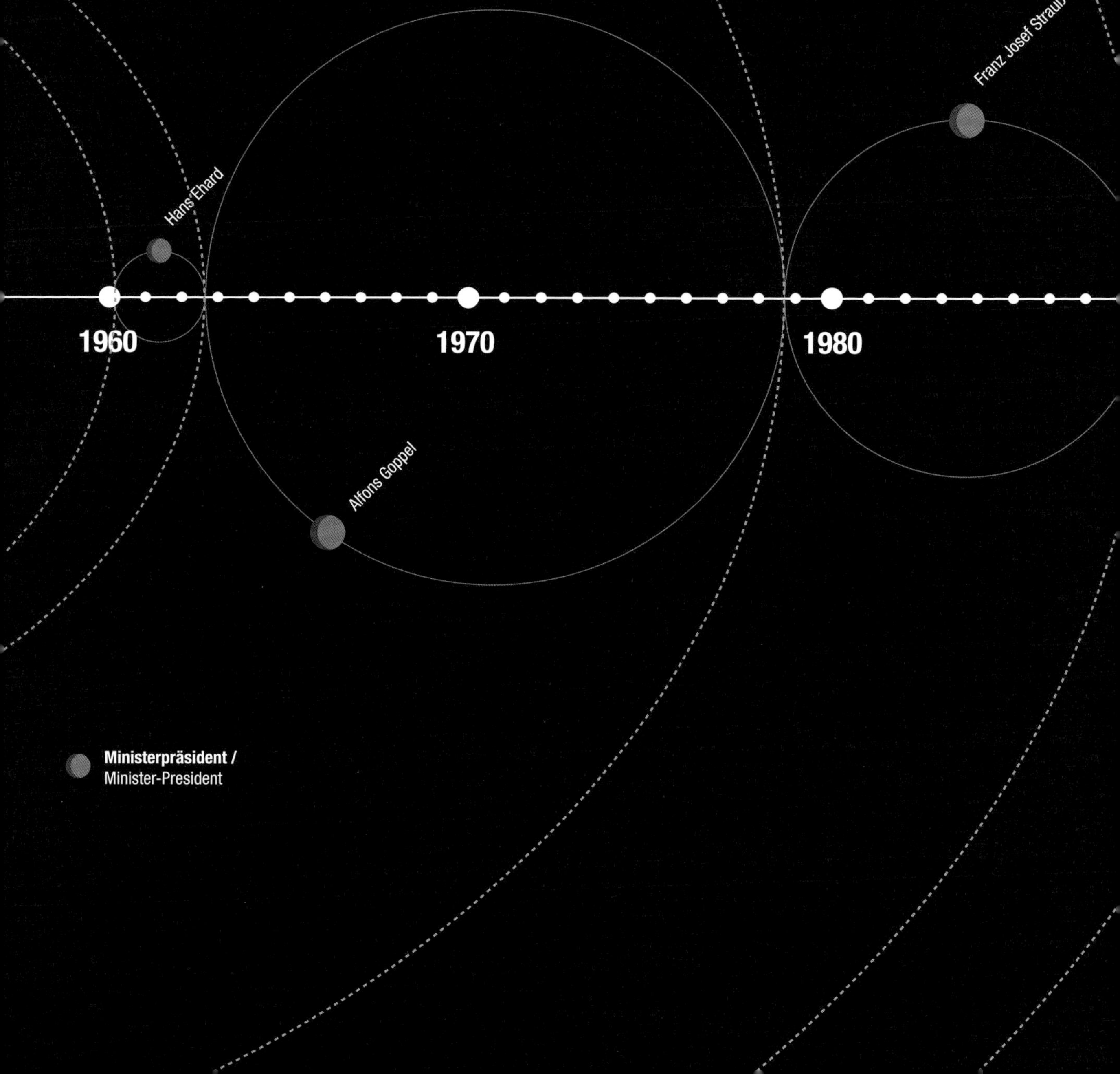

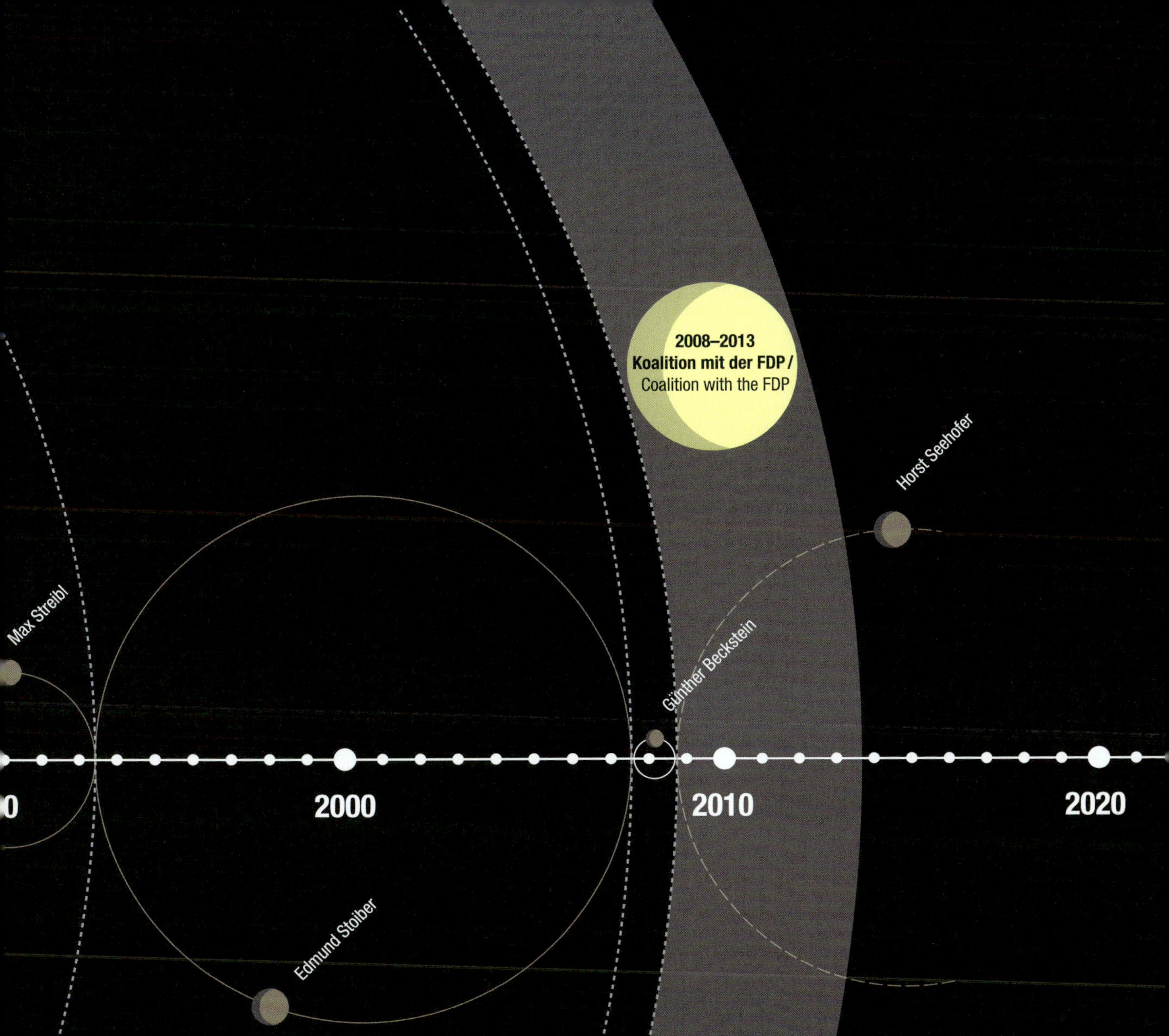

Seit 1962 hatte die Christlich-Soziale Union die absolute Mehrheit im Landtag und konnte damit alleine und übermächtig den Freistaat regieren. Ausnahme: 2008–2013 Koalition mit der FDP /
The Christian Social Union has for the most part enjoyed an absolute majority in the State Parliament, ruling supreme in Bavaria. Exception: From 2008–2013 there was a coalition government of CSU and FDP (Free Democratic Party).

Das ist ja die Höhe!
The sky's the limit!

Die höchsten Bauwerke im Freistaat /
The tallest buildings in Bavaria

München
Munich

Olympiaturm
Olympia Tower
291 m

Heizkraftwerk Süd
South Munich Cogeneration Power Station
176 m

Rest-Bayern
Rest of Bavaria

TÜRME UND ANLAGEN /
TOWERS AND PHYSICAL STRUCTURES

Fernmeldeturm Nürnberg
Nuremberg Telecommunications Tower
292,80 m

Windenergieanlage Winnberg 4
Winnberg 4 wind turbine
200 m

Werkskamin Industriepark Werk Gendorf
Gendorf Industrial Park smokestack
188 m

WOLKENKRATZER /
SKYSCRAPERS

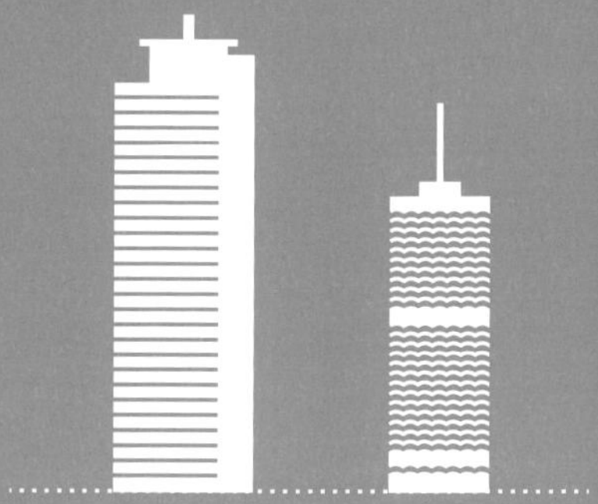

Business Tower Nürnberg /
Nuremberg
135 m

Dorint Augsburg
115 m

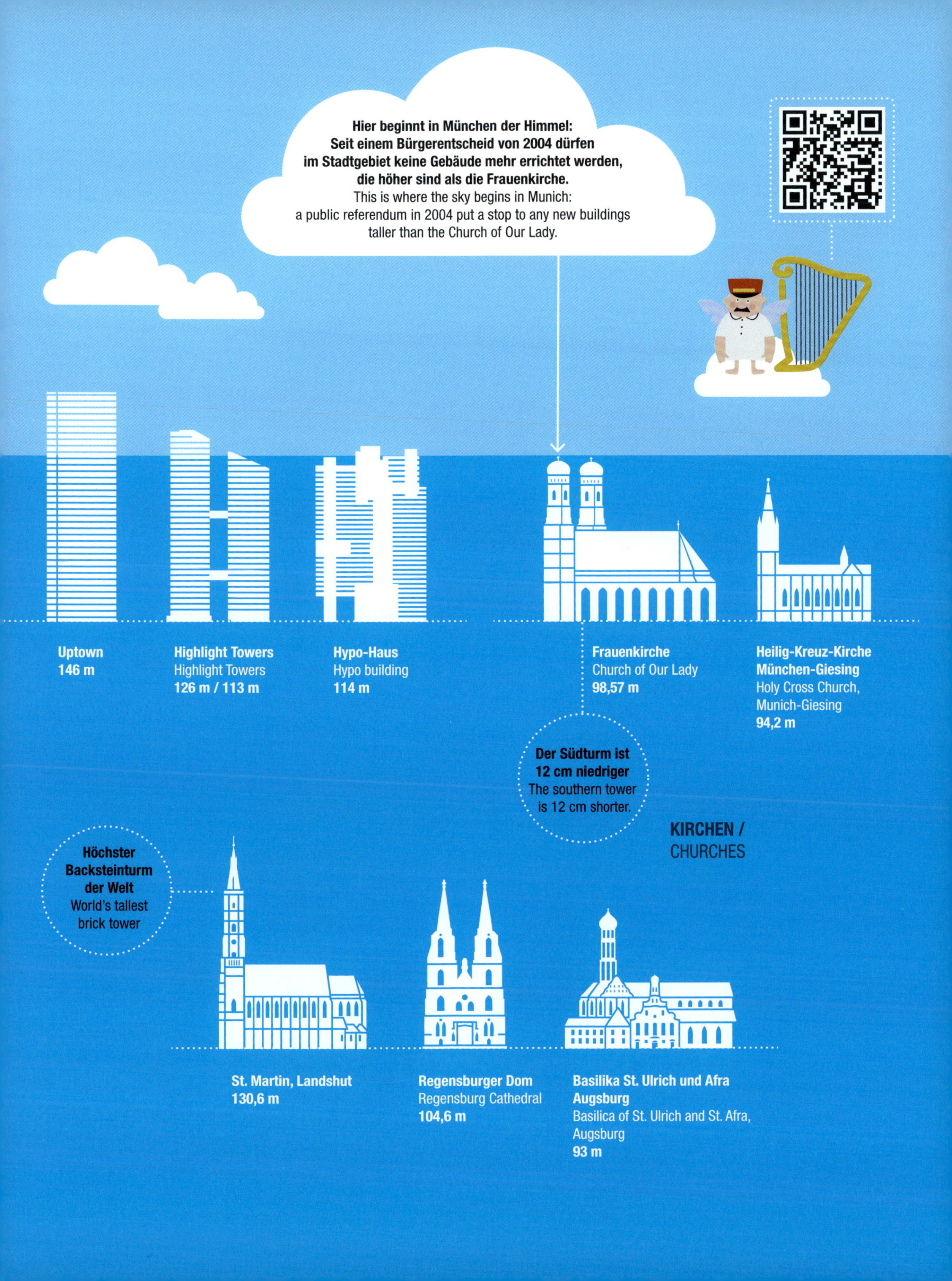
Hier beginnt in München der Himmel:
Seit einem Bürgerentscheid von 2004 dürfen
im Stadtgebiet keine Gebäude mehr errichtet werden,
die höher sind als die Frauenkirche.
This is where the sky begins in Munich:
a public referendum in 2004 put a stop to any new buildings
taller than the Church of Our Lady.
Uptown
146 m
Highlight Towers
Highlight Towers
126 m / 113 m
Hypo-Haus
Hypo building
114 m
Frauenkirche
Church of Our Lady
98,57 m
Heilig-Kreuz-Kirche
München-Giesing
Holy Cross Church,
Munich-Giesing
94,2 m
Der Südturm ist
12 cm niedriger
The southern tower
is 12 cm shorter.
KIRCHEN /
CHURCHES
Höchster
Backsteinturm
der Welt
World's tallest
brick tower
St. Martin, Landshut
130,6 m
Regensburger Dom
Regensburg Cathedral
104,6 m
Basilika St. Ulrich und Afra
Augsburg
Basilica of St. Ulrich and St. Afra,
Augsburg
93 m

Dem Himmel so nah
So close to heaven

Böse Zungen behaupten ja, die schönsten Berge der deutschen Alpen lägen in Österreich – der Gipfel der Frechheit. Hier sind 10 + 1 Gegenbeweise aus Oberbayern und Schwaben. / Malicious rumours have it that the most beautiful mountains in the German Alps are in Austria – the height of impertinence. Here are 10 + 1 proofs to the contrary from Upper Bavaria and Swabia.

Kraxelnde Sehenswürdigkeiten: die Huberbuam. Tipp: Immer nach oben schauen! / Clambering attractions: the extreme-climbing Huber brothers. Tip: Always look up!

Die höchsten Berge der anderen Regierungsbezirke
The highest mountains in the other administrative districts

Zugspitze 2.962 m – **Deutschlands höchste (und leider verbauteste) Spitze** Germany's highest (and unfortunately most developed) peak

Watzmann 2.713 m – **2014 zum „Schönsten Berg der Welt" gewählt** Elected "Most Beautiful Mountain in the World" in 2014

Hochkalter 2.607 m – **Leckerster Kuchen der Alpen auf der Blaueishütte** Most delicious cake in the Alps at the Blaueishütte cabin

Trettachspitze 2.595 m – **Das Allgäuer Matterhorn** The Matterhorn of the Allgäu region

Höfats 2.259 m – **Ein Edelweiß-Paradies** An Edelweiss paradise

Bergwacht Bayern
Bavarian Mountain Rescue Service

BERGWACHT BAYERN

4.200
ehrenamtliche Einsatzkräfte
volunteer rescue workers

Einsätze pro Jahr
Rescue missions per year

6.761 **Notfalleinsätze** emergency missions	**10** **Lawineneinsätze** avalanche rescues	**155** **Sucheinsätze** search missions	**81** **Todesfälle** deaths

Die gefährlichsten Sportarten
The most dangerous sports

3.073 **Skifahren** Skiing	**1.329** **Wandern** Hiking	**1.004** **Snowboarden** Snowboarding	**407** **Bergsteigen** Mountain climbing	**323** **Bergradeln** Mountain cycling

Soiernspitze 2.257 m
Ein Rückzugsort des „Kini"
A preferred retreat of "Kini" (King Ludwig II)

Berchtesgadener Hochthron 1.973 m
Der Kraftort für Schamanen
The place of power for shamans

Benediktenwand 1.801 m
Die Heimat der Steinböcke
Home of the ibexes

Wank 1.780 m
Der familienfreundliche Berg
The family-friendly mountain

Herzogstand 1.731 m
Der Lieblingsberg der Münchner
The Munich residents' favourite mountain

Fröttmaninger Müllberg refuse dump 75 m
Höhenrausch im Naherholungsgebiet
Intoxicating heights in an urban recreation area

Waldmeisterschaft
Sylvan supremacy

Das ist ja wohl der Wipfel: Bayerns Bäume / Hard to top: Bavaria's trees

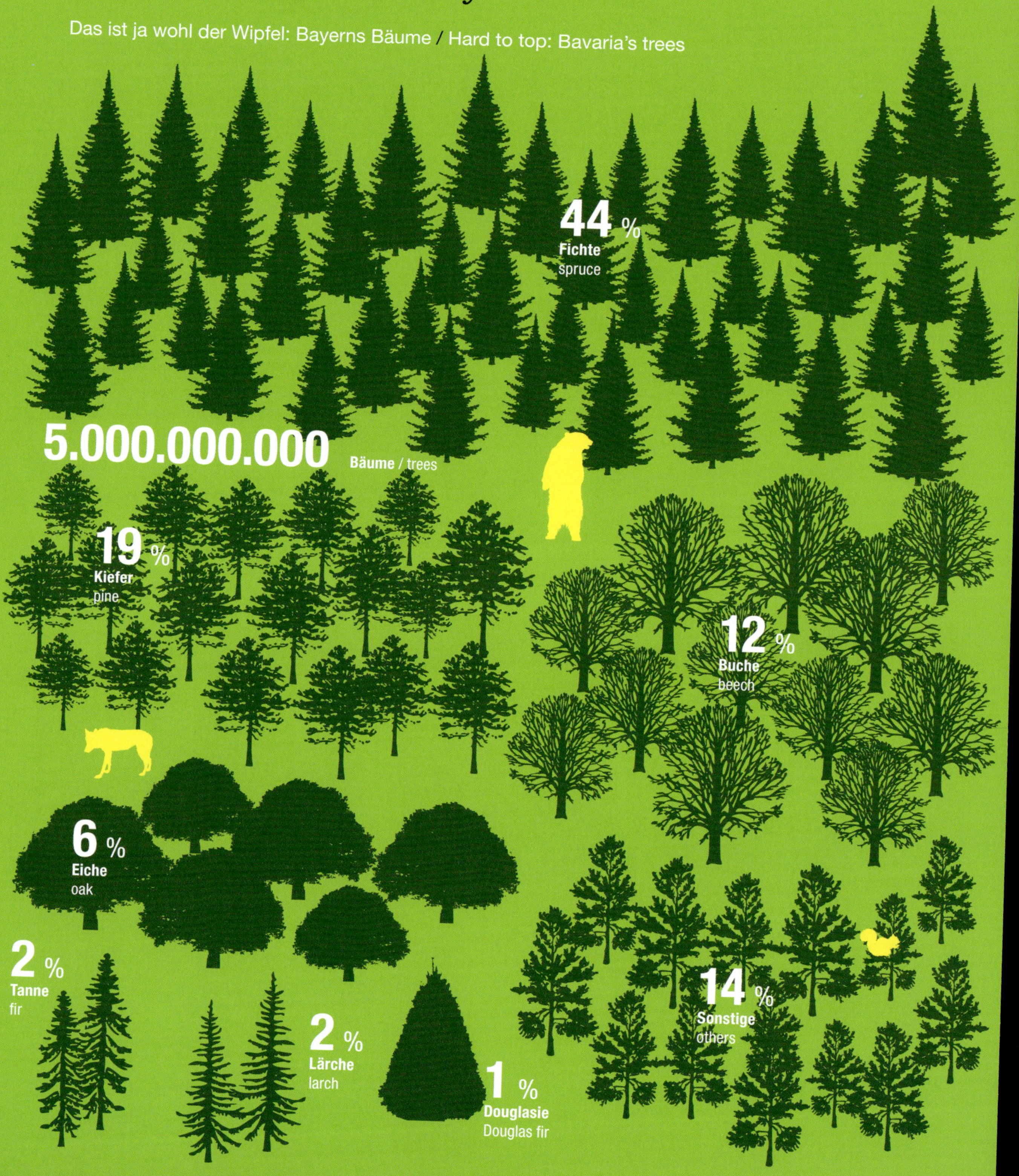

Holzvorrat / Wood reserves

31.536.000 m³

Zuwachs pro Jahr / annual growth

Damit könnte man jedes Jahr erneut eine 1 m breite und 11,66 m hohe Massivholzmauer rund um ganz Bayern (2.705 km) bauen.
This would be enough to build a new 1 m wide and 11.66 m high solid timber wall around the entire state of Bavaria each year (2,705 km).

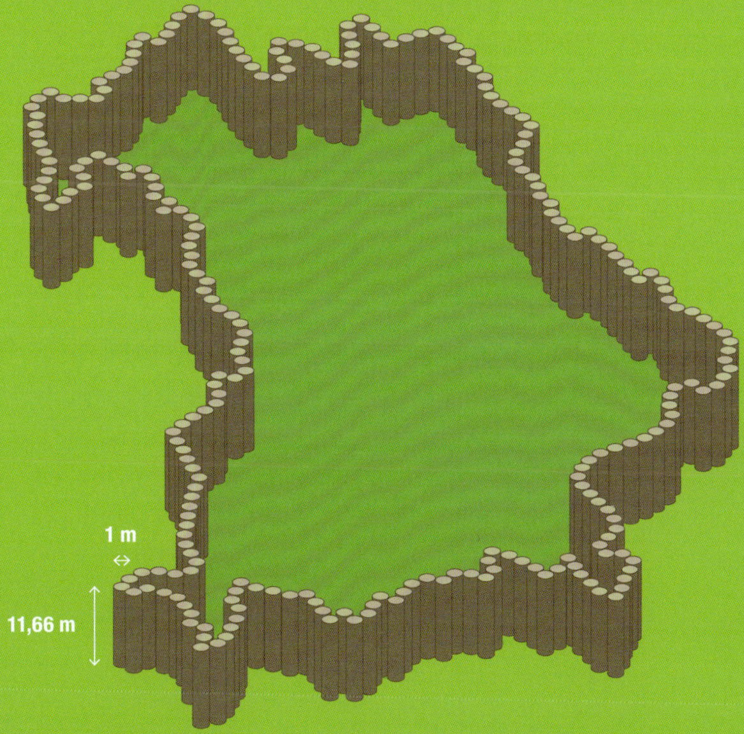

1 m³
Zuwachs pro Sekunde
growth per second

15.700.000 m³
Einschlag pro Jahr
annual felling

0,2 ha
Wald pro Einwohner
forest per inhabitant

Die Eigentümer der Wälder / Owners of the forests

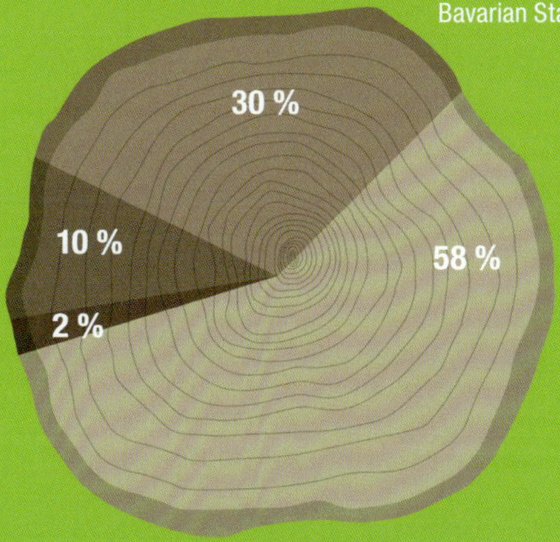

700.000
Waldbesitzer/-innen
forest owners

Aufs Korn genommen
In their sights

Mit Gewehr: Jagdszenen aus Niederbayern (und dem Rest des Freistaats) /
On their game: Hunting scenes from Lower Bavaria (and the rest of the state)

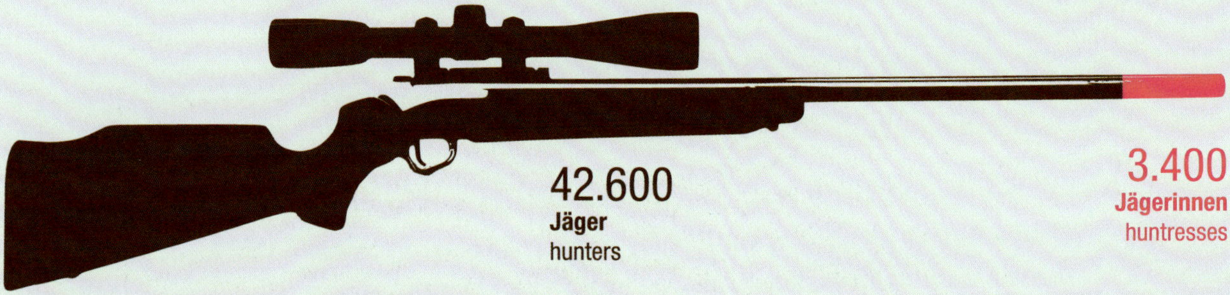

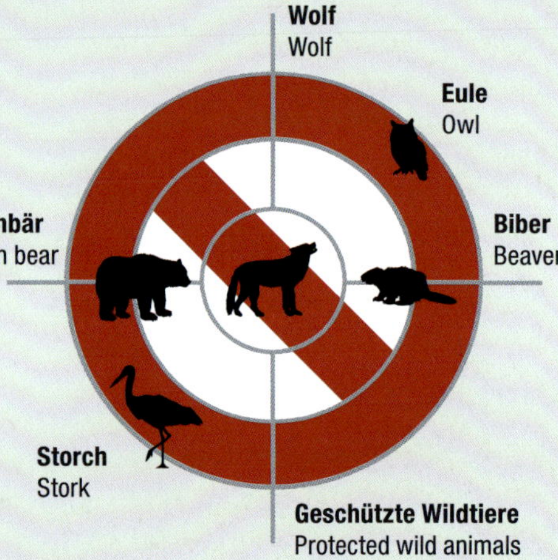

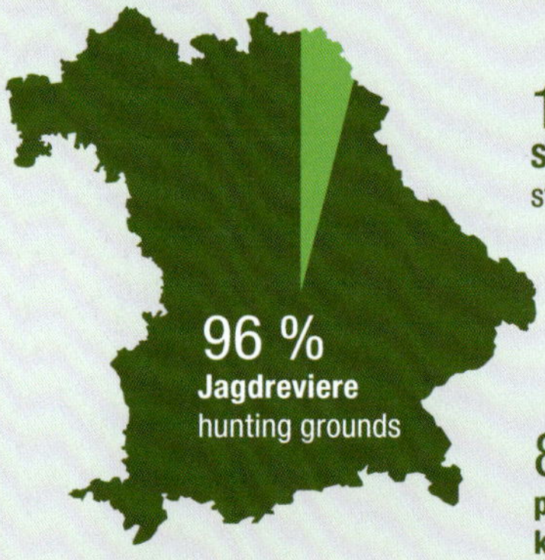

DER WILDSCHÜTZ / THE POACHER
GEORG „GIRGL“ JENNERWEIN

Hauptkarriere als Wilderer /
Main occupation: poacher

Nebenkarriere als Zitherspieler, Gstanzlsinger, Weiberheld, Bierdimpfl, Raufbold und Holzknecht /
Sidelines as zither player, “Gstanzl” singer, womaniser, tippler, ruffian and woodcutter

1848
in Haid bei / near **Holzkirchen**

1860
Sein Vater, ein Wilderer, wird von königlichen Jägern erschossen. /
His father, a poacher, is shot dead by royal hunters.

1877
Von hinten erschossen im Wald gefunden. /
Found in the woods, shot from behind.

Danach legendär als bayerischer Robin Hood. /
Thereafter legendary as Bavarian Robin Hood.

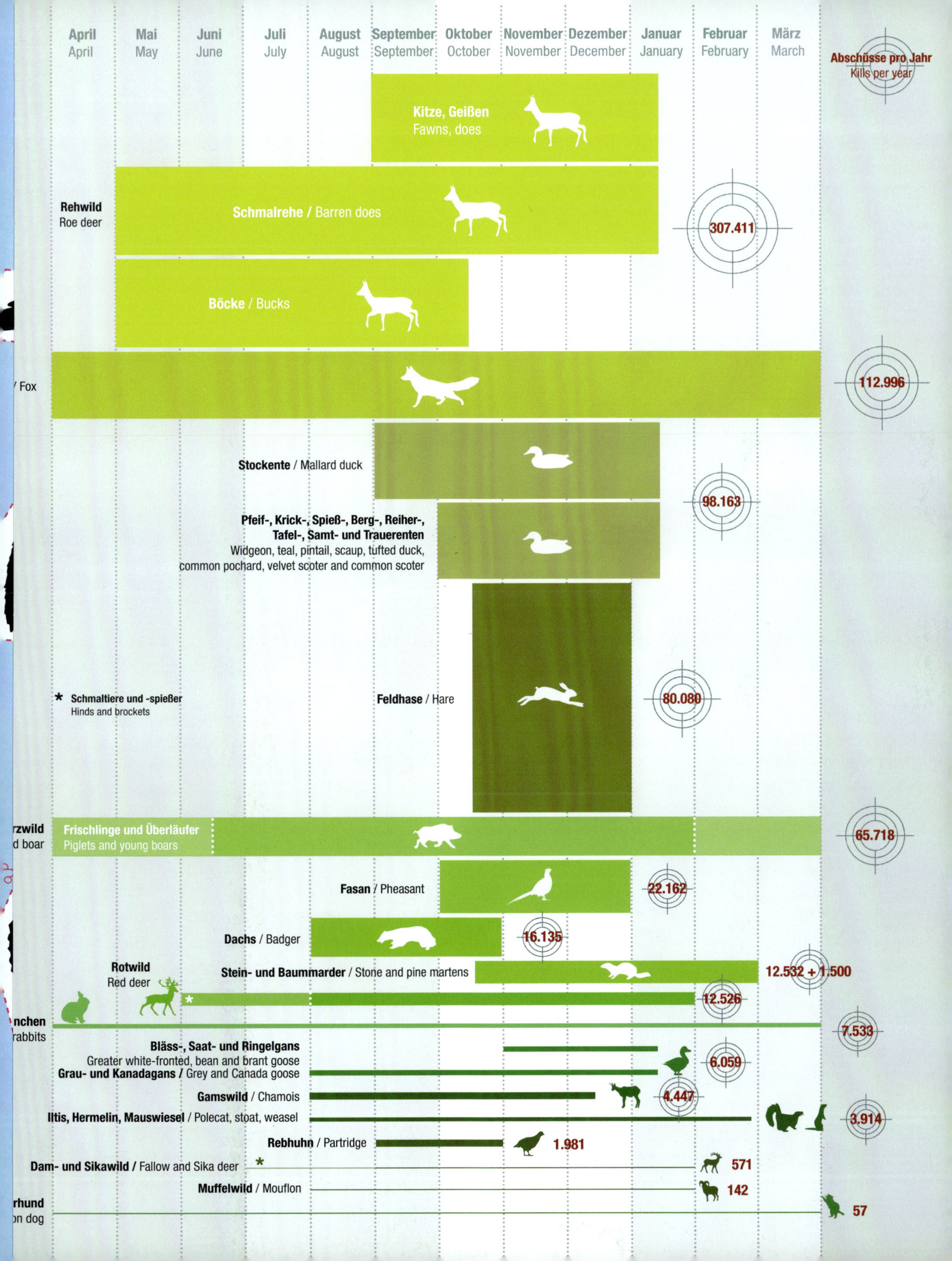

April
April
Mai
May
Juni
June
Juli
July
August
August
September
September
Oktober
October
November
November
Dezember
December
Januar
January
Februar
February
März
March
Abschüsse pro Jahr
Kills per year
Rehwild
Roe deer
Kitze, Geißen
Fawns, does
Schmalrehe / Barren does
Böcke / Bucks
307.411
/ Fox
112.996
Stockente / Mallard duck
Pfeif-, Krick-, Spieß-, Berg-, Reiher-,
Tafel-, Samt- und Trauerenten
Widgeon, teal, pintail, scaup, tufted duck,
common pochard, velvet scoter and common scoter
98.163
* Schmaltiere und -spießer
Hinds and brockets
Feldhase / Hare
80.080
rzwild
d boar
Frischlinge und Überläufer
Piglets and young boars
65.718
Fasan / Pheasant
22.162
Dachs / Badger
16.135
Stein- und Baummarder / Stone and pine martens
12.532 + 1.500
Rotwild
Red deer
*
12.526
nchen
rabbits
7.533
Bläss-, Saat- und Ringelgans
Greater white-fronted, bean and brant goose
Grau- und Kanadagans / Grey and Canada goose
6.059
Gamswild / Chamois
4.447
Iltis, Hermelin, Mauswiesel / Polecat, stoat, weasel
3.914
Rebhuhn / Partridge
1.981
Dam- und Sikawild / Fallow and Sika deer
*
571
Muffelwild / Mouflon
142
rhund
on dog
57

Host an Vogel?
Have you gone batty?

Die Bayern lieben ihre Tiere, und sie lieben das Schimpfen. Am liebsten kombinieren sie diese beiden Leidenschaften – mit animalischen Kosenamen für ihre Mitmenschen. Komplimente sind das eher selten. / The Bavarians love their animals, and they love scolding. But they're really in their element when they combine the two – with animal-based nicknames for their fellow human beings. These are rarely flattering.

Spinner
Spinner
Rindviech
Stupid cow
Ochs
Ox
Kalb
Calf
Kuh
Cow
Schaf
Sheep
Hirsch
Deer
Protz
Toad
Sau
Sow
Ferkel
Pig
Saubär
Boar
Wildsau
Wild sow
Huhn
Hen
Gockel
Cock
Schnepfe
Snipe
Gans
Goose
Uhu
Owl
Kauz
Owl
Haubentaucher
Great Crested Grebe
Amsel
Blackbird
Geier
Vulture

… die größten Kartoffeln
… the biggest potatoes

Die Landwirtschaft in Bayern – ein Bauerzustand / Farming in Bavaria – the order of the day

FLÄCHENNUTZUNG / LAND USE (2010)

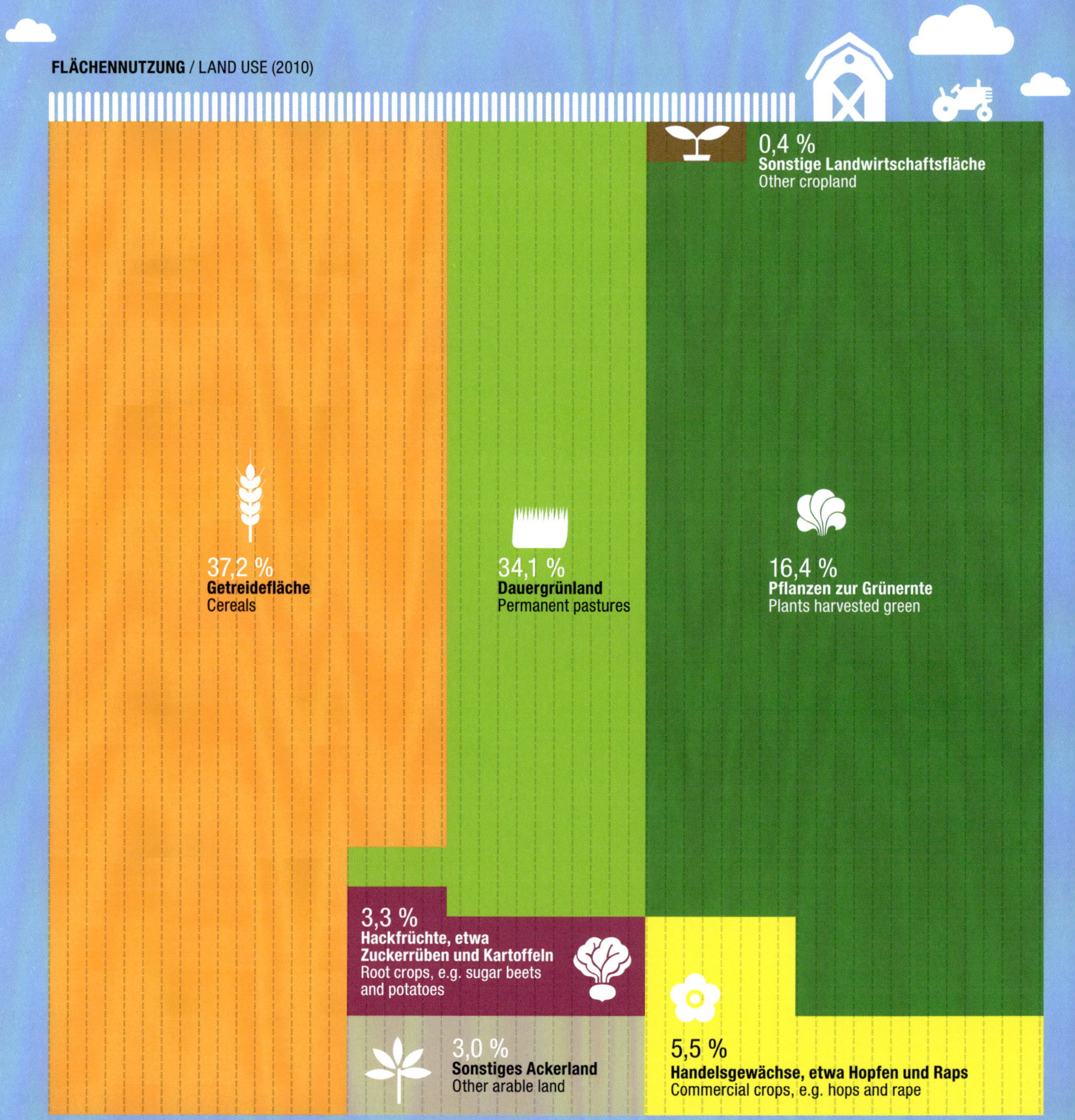

FBERICHTERSTATTUNG
E FARM REPORT

	Zahl der Höfe Number of farms	**davon: unter 5 ha** thereof: under 5 ha	**mehr als 100 ha** more than 100 ha
1979	274.273	78.231	569
1999	154.189	28.244	1.976
2010	97.735	4.035	4.057

BVENTIONEN
BSIDIES

1,04 Milliarden / billion €

erhielten die Agrarbetriebe in Bayern 2013 insgesamt an EU-Subventionen.
in EU-subsidies was received by agricultural operations in Bavaria in 2009.

OLOGISCHER LANDBAU
GANIC FARMING

6.437
Betriebe / operations
197.893 ha

Anteil der Biomilch in Molkereien
Ratio of organic milk produced by dairies

Anteil der Bio-Tiere an Bayerns Gesamtbestand
Ratio of organically raised livestock in Bavaria's agricultural operations

5,6 %
Rinder / Cattle

0,8 %
Schweine / Pigs

5,8 %
Geflügel / Poultry

9,5 %
Schafe / Sheep

40,7 %
Ziegen / Goats

DAS LIEBE VIEH
LIVESTOCK

3.253.900
Rinder, Kühe und Kälber
Steers, cows and calves

Eine Milchkuh gibt 6.490 kg Milch pro Jahr.
A milk cow produces 6.490 kg milk per year.

3.549.000
Schweine und Zuchtsauen
Pigs and breeding sows

11.055.800
Legehennen und Masthühner
Laying hens and broiler chickens

1,04 Milliarden Eier pro Jahr
billion eggs per year

332.300
Schafe
Sheep

3.670
Ziegen
Goats

Prost, Mahlzeit!
To your health!

Was ein Durchschnittsbayer jeden Tag so verdrückt /
What the average Bavarian downs in one day

Mittelwert
Average amount

4.242 g **Männer** Men
3.739 g **Frauen** Women

	Männer / Men	Frauen / Women
Brot Bread	162 g	120 g
Backwaren Baked goods	50 g	37 g
Getreide und Getreideerzeugnisse Cereal and cereal products	37 g	36 g
Getreidegerichte Cereal dishes	57 g	46 g
Gemüse, Pilze, Hülsenfrüchte Vegetables, mushrooms, legumes	106 g	125 g
Gemüsegerichte Vegetable dishes	140 g	145 g
Kartoffeln und Kartoffelerzeugnisse Potatoes and potato products	74 g	61 g
Kartoffelgerichte Potato dishes	12 g	9 g
Obst und Obsterzeugnisse Fruit and fruit products	214 g	269 g
Fette und Öle Fats and oils	23 g	17 g
Milch und Milchmischgetränke Milk and milk drinks	111 g	96 g
Milcherzeugnisse Dairy products	76 g	82 g
Käse und Quark Cheese and quark	39 g	37 g
Milchspeisen Milk dishes	16 g	15 g
Eier Eggs	12 g	9 g

Eierspeisen Egg dishes	7 g	6 g
Fleisch Meat	41 g	24 g
Fleischerzeugnisse und Wurstwaren Meat products and sausages	71 g	32 g
Fleischgerichte Meat dishes	54 g	29 g
Fisch und Fischerzeugnisse und Krustentiere Fish, seafood and shellfish	15 g	13 g
Fischgerichte Fish dishes	13 g	11 g
Suppen und Eintöpfe Soups and stews	99 g	88 g
Süßwaren Sweets	54 g	50 g
Knabberartikel Savoury snacks	7 g	5 g
Wasser Water	1097 g	1081 g
Kaffee und Tee (grün, schwarz) Coffee and tea (green, black)	505 g	478 g
Kräuter- und Früchtetee Herbal and fruit tea	147 g	329 g
Obstsaft und Nektare Fruit juice and nectar	315 g	299 g
Limonaden Lemonades	282 g	93 g
Bier Beer	357 g	59 g
Wein, Sekt Wine, sparkling wine	48 g	40 g
Spirituosen Spirits	4 g	1 g
Alkopops, alkoholische Cocktails Alcopops, alcoholic cocktails	4 g	3 g

178 g
Lebensmittel schmeißt der Bayer täglich weg
is the amount of food the average Bavarian throws away every day.

59 %
der Männer sind übergewichtig
of the men are overweight.

41 %
der Frauen sind übergewichtig
of the women are overweight.

An guadn!
Enjoy!

Aufgebrezelt: Bayerische Erzeugnisse unter EU-Schutz / Pepped up: Bavarian products under EU protection

2010
Hopfen aus der Hallertau
Hops from the Hallertau

2012
Spalter Hopfen
Spalt hops

2013
Bamberger Hörnla
Bamberg potato

2007
Bayerischer Meerrettich
Bavarian horseradish

2009
Schwäbische Maultaschen
Swabian Maultaschen

2012
Schwäbische Spätz
Swabian spaetzle

2001
Bayerisches Bier
Bavarian beer

1998
Kulmbacher Bier
Kulmbach beer

1998
Mainfranken Bier
Mainfranken beer

2010
Münchener Bier
Munich beer

1998
Reuther Bier
Reuth beer

1998
Hofer Bier
Hof beer

2011
Hofer Rindfleischwurst
Hof beef sausage

2003
Nürnberger Rostbratwürste
Nuremberg bratwursts

2011
Bayerisches Rindfleisch
Bavarian beef

1997
Allgäuer Bergkäse
Allgäu mountain cheese

1997
Allgäuer Emmentaler
Allgäu mountain cheese

1996
Nürnberger Lebkuch
Nuremberg Lebkuche

2012
Abensberger Spargel
Abensberg asparagus

2013
Fränkischer Spargel
Franconian asparagus

2010
Schrobenhausener Spargel
Schrobenhausen asparagus

2012
Aischgründer Karpfen
Aischgrund carp

2012
Franken-Karpfen
Franconian carp

2002
Oberpfälzer Karpfe
Upper Palatinate carp

1998
Schwäbisch-Hällisches Qualitätsschweinefleisch
Swabian-Hall quality pork

2014
Bayerische Brezn
Bavarian pretzel

geschützte geographische Angabe (g.g.A.)
protected geographical indication (PGI)

geschützte Ursprungsbezeichnung (g.U.)
protected designation of origin (PDO)

September–April
Karpfen werden nur in den Monaten mit „r“ angeboten – zumeist gebacken.
Carps are offered only in the months with “r” – mostly baked.
24.6.
Ende der Spargelsaison („Kirschen rot, Spargel tot.“)
End of the asparagus season (“The cherry is red, and the asparagus is dead.”)
1313
1. urkundliche Erwähnung
1st documentation
20–25 g
8–10 cm
1516
Erlass des Bayerischen Reinheitsgebots durch Herzog Wilhelm IV. von Bayern
William IV, Duke of Bavaria, issues the well-known Bavarian Purity Law.
UNTERFRANKEN LOWER FRANCONIA
OBERFRANKEN UPPER FRANCONIA
MITTELFRANKEN MIDDLE FRANCONIA
OBERPFALZ UPPER PALATINATE
NIEDERBAYERN LOWER BAVARIA
SCHWABEN SWABIA
OBERBAYERN UPPER BAVARIA
430 ha
Anbaufläche
cultivating area
150–400 g
Hopfen werden pro hl Bier verarbeitet. / of hops are processed per hl of beer.
15.500 ha
Anbaufläche
cultivating area
1831
1. urkundliche Erwähnung
1st documentation
40.000 t
Spätzleproduktion in Deutschland pro Jahr
Annual poduction of spaetzle in Germany
900 ha
Anbaufläche
cultivating area
600
Spargelanbauer
asparagus growers
4 Monate Mindestalter
4 month minimum age
Erfinder / Inventor
Anton Nepomuk Pfannenbrenner
11.02.1839
Erstverkaufstag / First day of sale

Schwarzbuch Weißwurst
The black book on the white sausage

Weil es eben nicht wurst ist, was in der Wurst ist: Wie die Leibspeise der Bayern gemacht, erwärmt und gegessen wird (nach Münchens bestem Metzger, Magnus Bauch) / Because only the best is good enough for the wurst, here's how Bavaria's favourite food is made, heated and eaten (according to Munich's top butcher, Magnus Bauch)

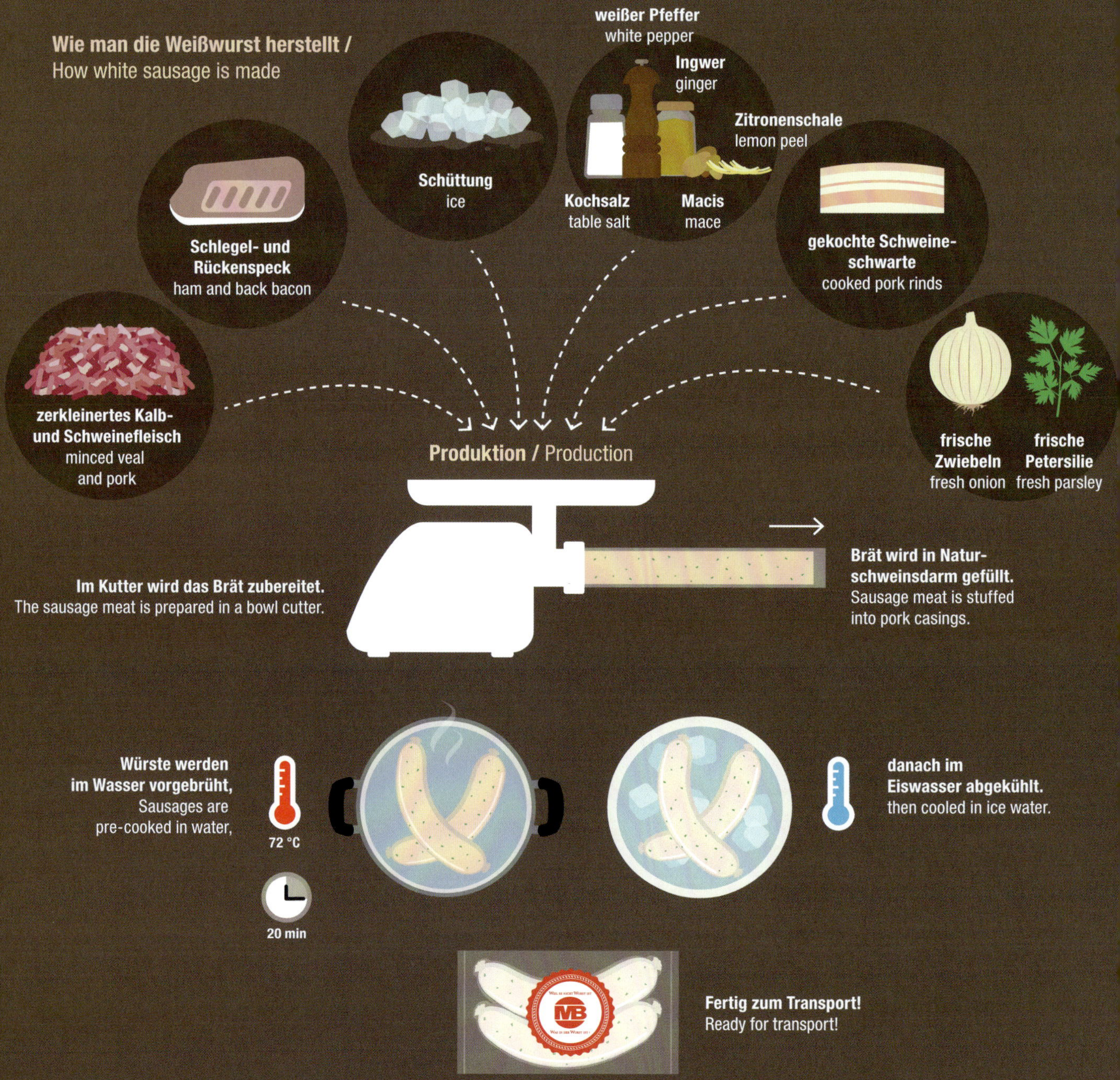

Wie man die Weißwurst erwärmt / How to heat up white sausage

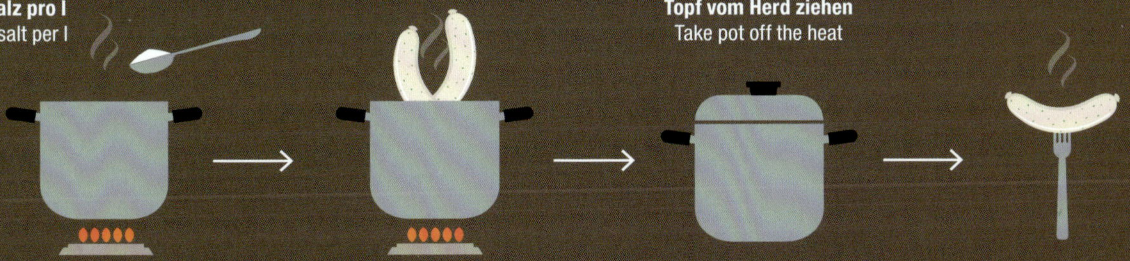

1 EL Salz pro l
1 tbsp salt per l

Wasser kochen.
Boil water.

Weißwürste hineingeben, einzeln oder paarweise (bei dreien oder mehr drohen die mittleren zu platzen).
Put white sausages into the water, individually or in pairs (if three or more, the ones in the middle might burst).

Topf vom Herd ziehen
Take pot off the heat

Deckel drauf
Put lid on

Nach 20 min sind sie fertig.
They are ready in 20 min.

Wie man die Weißwurst isst / How to eat white sausage

① **Mit der Gabel anstechen,**
Pierce with fork,

② **einmal quer in der Mitte durchschneiden,**
cut in half crosswise,

③ **Wursthälften der Länge nach aufschneiden,**
cut each half down the middle lengthwise,

④ **mit der Gabel aus der Pelle ziehen und essen.**
pull out of casing with fork and eat.

⑤ **Dazu Weißbier, Brezn und süßer Senf.**
Ideal with wheat beer, pretzels and sweet mustard.

Wie man die Weißwurst NICHT isst / How NOT to eat white sausage

- **kalt** cold
- **gegrillt** grilled
- **angebraten** fried
- **gebacken** baked
- **paniert** breaded
- **mit der Hand** with your hands
- **mit der Haut** with the casing
- **zuzeln** by sucking out of casing
- **nach 12 Uhr mittags *** after 12 o'clock noon *

* **Die Regel stammt aus Zeiten ohne Kühlschrank.** / This rule comes from the days before refrigeration.

Bier gewinnt
There's nothing like beer!

Kein Volk dieser Erde ist so stolz auf seine Lieblingsdroge wie die Bayern auf ihren Gerstensaft. Und das auch noch mit Recht. Prost! / No people on earth is as proud of its favourite drug as the Bavarians are of their beer. And you can't blame them. Cheers!

BAYERISCHER GESAMTBIERAUSSTOSS 2013
TOTAL BAVARIAN BEER PRODUCTION IN 2013

24 **Mio.** / mil. **hl**

1,7 **Mio.** / million **hl**
alkoholfreies Bier
non-alcoholic beer

22,3 **Mio.** / million **hl**
Vollbier
Vollbier (11 to 14% extract)

17,9 Mio. / million **hl**
Bayerischer Gesamtbierabsatz im Inland 2013
Total domestic sales of Bavarian beer in 2013

4,4 Mio. / million **hl**
Im Ausland
sold abroad

Damit könnte man die Allianz-Arena zu 82 % füllen.
This quantity would fill 82% of the Allianz Arena.

215 l
Geschätzter durchschnittlicher Bierkonsum pro Kopf pro Jahr (bei über 16-jährigen Bayern)
Estimated average per capita beer consumption per year (amongst Bavarians over 16 years of age)

DIE KEHRSEITE DES BIERDECKELS – BAYERISCHE KRANKENSTATISTIK 2012
THE OTHER SIDE OF THE BEER MAT – BAVARIAN ILLNESS STATISTICS IN 2012

53.002
Patienten mit alkoholbedingten Krankheiten
patients with alcohol-related illnesses

23.082 **davon wegen akuten Rausches**
thereof due to acute intoxication
5.683 **davon unter 20 Jahre alt**
thereof under 20 years of age

ERTEILUNG DER DREI BELIEBTESTEN SORTEN
EOGRAPHIC DISTRIBUTION OF THE THREE MOST POPULAR BEER TYPES

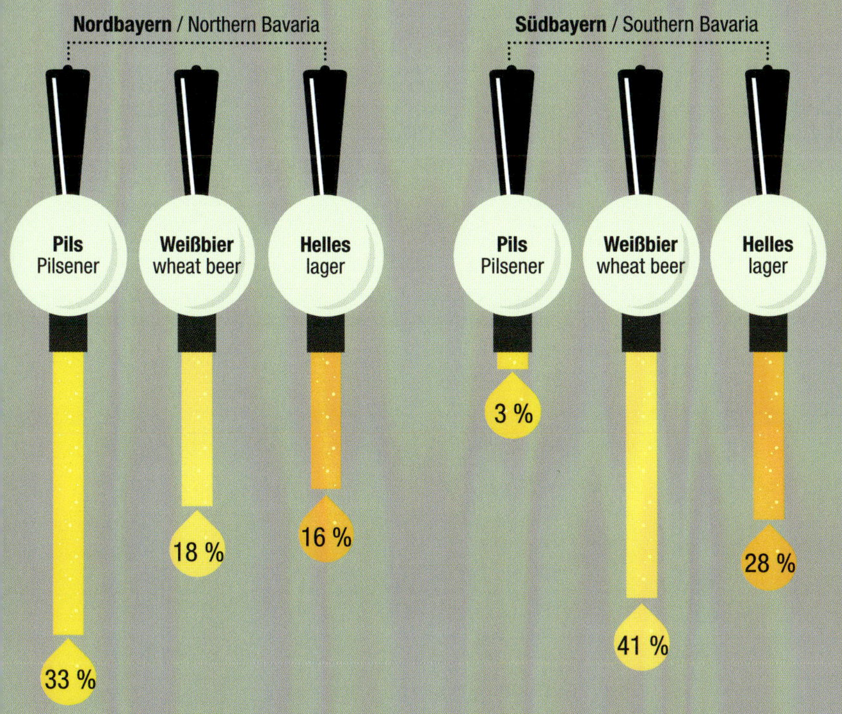

ENERGIE
ENERGY

Der Gesamtbierabsatz Bayerns 2013 könnte theoretisch ein Jahr lang 1.108.603 Menschen ernähren – mehr als alle erwachsenen Münchner.
The total Bavarian beer sales in 2013 could theoretically feed 1,108,603 people for one year – more than the entire adult population of Munich.

Tag des deutschen Bieres
German Beer Day

BRAUEREIEN IN DEUTSCHLAND
BREWERIES IN GERMANY

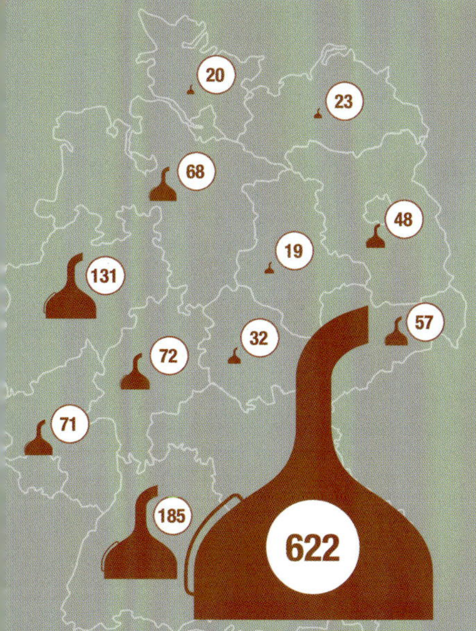

DIE WELTGRÖSSTEN BIERPRODUZENTEN IN MIO. HL
THE WORLD'S BIGGEST BEER PRODUCERS

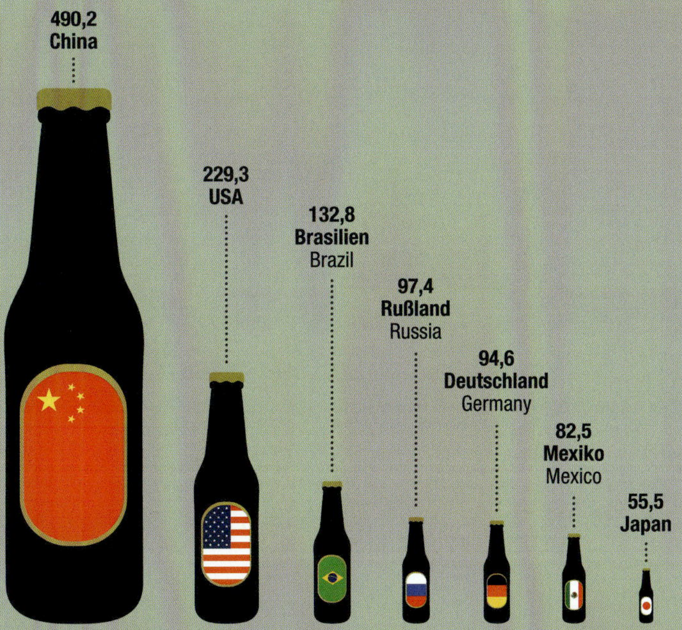

Im Land der Schenkelklopfer

In the land of the knee slappers

Mit dem Schuhplattler, traditionell in Tracht aufgeführt, buhlten die Tänzer einst um die Herzen ihrer Angebeteten – heute erobern sie damit vor allem die der Touristen. / With the Schuhplattler dance, traditionally performed in folk costume, men once courted their sweethearts – and today conquer the hearts of tourists.

Im Paradiesgarten
In the Garden of Eden

Alles außer Äpfel und Schlangen: Was einen Biergarten zu einem Biergarten macht. / Everything but apples and snakes: What makes a beergarden a beergarden

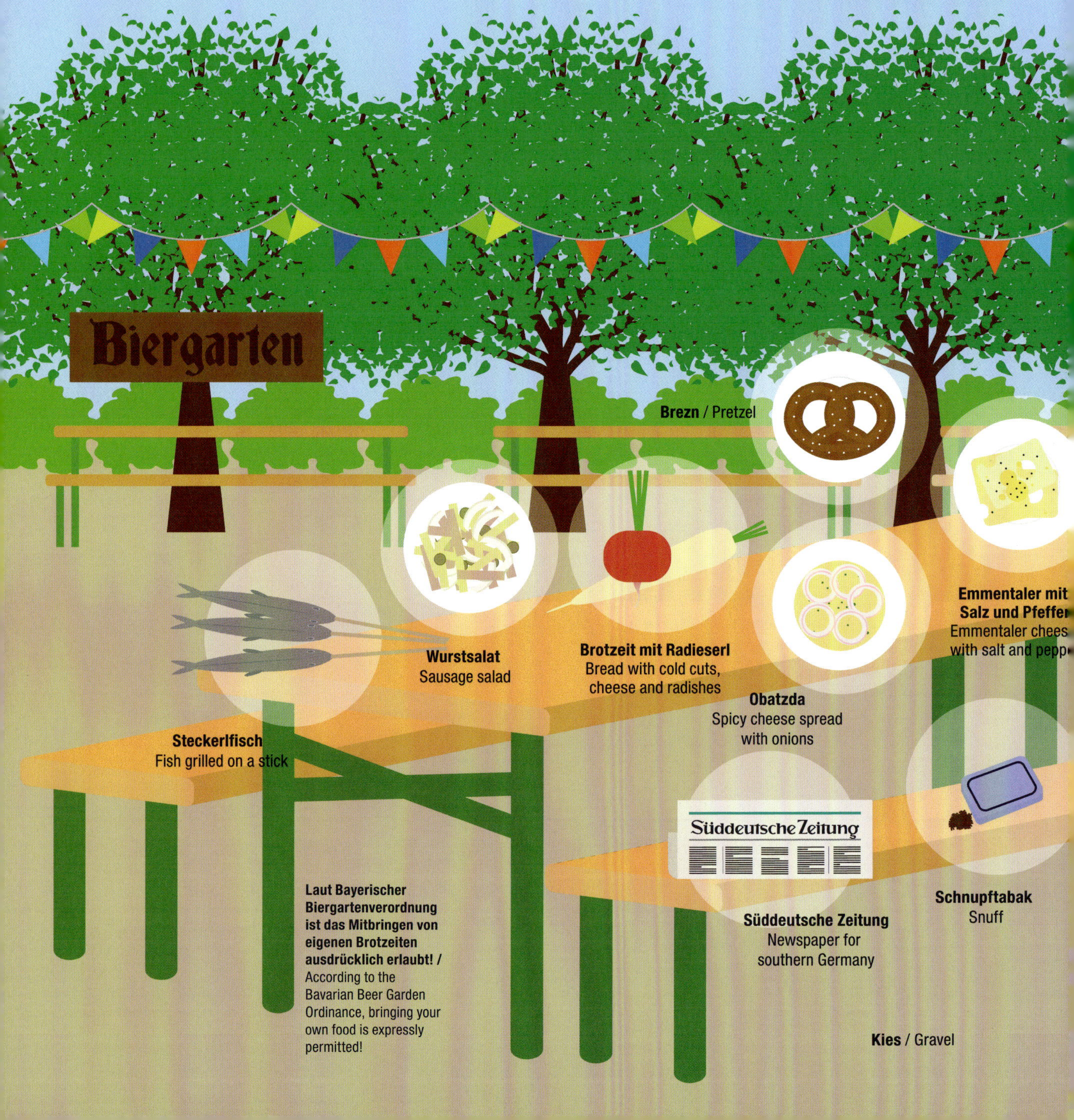

Kirchturm / Church tower
Maibaum / Maypole
Dirndlbluse mit Puffärmeln und Ausschnitt (im Idealfall: Holz vor der Hüttn) / Dirndl blouse with puffed sleeves and a low neckline (best case scenario: with a well-endowed wearer)
Dirndlkleid mit vorne geschnürtem Mieder / Dirndl dress with front-laced bodice
Schafkopfen Trick-taking card game
Charivari / Chain with charms worn across the bodice
Helles Lager
Radler Shandy with lager
Russ Shandy with wheat beer
Weißbier Wheat beer
Obstler Fruit brandy
Schleife (links gebunden heißt: Trägerin ist noch zu haben) / Bow (tied on the left: the wearer is still available)
Schürze / Apron
Dirndlkleid / Folk dress
„Zamperl" (Dackel) / Dachshund

O'zapft is!
Bottoms up!

Maßlos maßvoll: zwei Wochen lang die größte Party der Welt, das Oktoberfest /
Barrels of fun: for two weeks the biggest party in the world, the Oktoberfest

BIERAUSSCHANK IN DEN GROSSEN BIERZELTEN
BEER SERVED IN THE BIG BEER TENTS:

Wochentags Weekdays	**Samstags und an Sonn- und Feiertagen** Saturday, Sunday and holidays
10–22:30 **Uhr** / h	9–22:30 **Uhr** / h

Oktober / October 1810

1. Oktoberfest anlässlich der Hochzeit von Kronprinz Ludwig und Prinzessin Therese
1st Oktoberfest celebrating the wedding of Crown Prince Ludwig and Princess Therese

Hofbräu-Festzelt

größte Festhalle (inkl. Biergarten) mit über 11.000 Sitzplätzen
biggest banquet hall (incl. beer garden) with over 11,000 seats

15 %
der Maßkrüge sind nicht voll eingeschenkt (Unterschank).
of the beer mugs are not completely filled.

15 mm
Unterschank sind erlaubt.
empty space from the top of the beer mug is allowed.

1,5 s
durchschnittliche Einschankzeit für eine Maß
average filling time for a one-litre mug

81.000
Bierkrüge wurden 2013 den Andenkenjägern abgenommen.
beer mugs were reclaimed from souvenir hunters in 2013.

Essensbilanz / Food balance sheet **(2013)**

78.216
Schweinshaxen
pork knuckles

115.015
Paar Schweinswürstl
pairs of pork sausages

508.958
Hendl
chickens

116
Ochsen
oxen

85
Kälber
calves

410 t
Speisereste, Knochen
food scraps, bones

Infrastruktur / Infrastructure

31 ha
Fläche
floor area

14
große Zelte
big tents

21
kleine Zelte
small tents

8.000
Festangestellte
permanent staff members

4.000
wechselnde Arbeitskräfte
temporary workers

95
Gastronomiebetriebe
food establishments

80
Fahrgeschäfte
amusement park rides

114.000
Sitzplätze
seats

60
Flöhe im Flohzirkus
fleas in the flea circus

848 m
Toiletten-Stehplätze
pissoirs

1.410
Toiletten-Sitzplätze
toilet seats

26
behindertengerechte Toiletten
disabled toilets

Verbrauch / Consumption

2,73 Mio. / mil. **kWh**
Strom / electricity

43 km
Kabel / cable

114.612 m³
Wasser / water

Herkunft der Oktoberfestbesucher
Countries of origin of Oktoberfest visitors

72 % **Bayern**
Bavaria

9 % **Rest Deutschlands**
The rest of Germany

19 % **Ausland**
Abroad

Kuriosa / Curiosities

Berühmtester Hilfsarbeiter auf der Wiesn
Most famous worker at the Wiesn
Albert Einstein

Der Münchner Oberbürgermeister zapft traditionell das erste Bierfass an und läutet damit den Beginn der Wiesn ein.
Munich's Lord Mayor traditionally taps the first barrel, kicking off the beginning of the Oktoberfest.

Größter Fauxpas („Izapft os" statt „Ozapft is")
Biggest faux pas (He said "Izapft os" instead of "Ozapft is"): Erich Kiesl (1978)

Schnellster Anzapfer / Fastest barrel tapper
Christian Ude (2 Schläge / strikes, **2009)**

„2 Maß sind nicht zu viel für Autofahrer."
"2 litres of beer is not too much for a driver."
(Günther Beckstein, 2008)

Weltmusikantenstadl
Worldwide hit parade

New York, Rio, Rosenheim: Bayerische Musiker begeistern im Bierzelt wie im Konzertsaal. Und zwar global! / New York, Rio, Rosenheim: Bavarian musicians are popular both in the beer tent and on the concert stage. All over the world!

Die Krüge hoch! Diese 15 Wiesn-Hits spielt die Münchner Zwietracht bei jedem Auftritt.
Cheers! The Münchner Zwietracht play these 15 Oktoberfest hits at every show.

Auf Welttournee: Bayerische Musiker und ihre exotischen Auftritte (jeweils 15 ausgewählte Orte)
On world tour: Bavarian musicians and their exotic gigs (15 selected venues for each)

MÜNCHNER ZWIETRACHT
MÜNCHNER PHILHARMONIKER
REGENSBURGER DOMSPATZEN
LABRASSBANDA

Die Notenbesten
The top of the pops

DAS BLECHERNSTE HOBBY
THE BRASSIEST HOBBY
120.000 bayerische Blasmusiker in 2.500 Kapellen und Vereinen
120,000 Bavarian brass players in 2,500 bands and clubs

ERSTE WESTDEUTSCHE BAND AUF DDR-TOURNEE
FIRST WEST GERMAN BAND TO TOUR EAST GERMANY
Spider Murphy Gang (1983)

EINST NUMMER EINS IN THAILAND
ONCE NUMBER ONE IN THAILAND
„You drive me crazy“ von / by **Daniel Küblböck**

DER GRÖSSTE HIT
THE BIGGEST HIT
„Mambo No. 5“ vom Münchner Lou Bega, die erfolgreichste deutsche Musikproduktion aller Zeiten / by Lou Bega of Munich, the most successful German music production of all time

DAS LEGENDÄRSTE STUDIO
THE MOST LEGENDARY STUDIO
Musicland in München / Munich **(Rolling Stones, Led Zeppelin, Iggy Pop, Freddie Mercury, Donna Summer etc.)**

DAS GRÖSSTE FESTIVAL IN BAYERN
THE BIGGEST FESTIVAL IN BAVARIA
„Rock im Park“ in Nürnberg / Nuremberg: **70.000 Besucher** / visitors

OSCAR-PREISTRÄGER
OSCAR-WINNERS

Rolf Zehetbauer, Cabaret 1972
(Bestes Szenenbild
Best Art Direction**)**

Peter Denz, 1996
(flackerfreie Videokamera
Technical Achievement Award: development of a flicker-free color video camera**)**

Thomas Stellmach, Quest 1997
(bester Animierter Kurzfilm
Best Animated Short Film**)**

Florian Gallenberger, Quiero ser 2001
(Bester Kurzfilm
Best Short Film**)**

Johannes Saam, 2014
(Preis für technische Verdienste
Technical Achievement Award**)**

Firma ARRI, 2011, 2002, 1992, 1982
(Kameratechnik
Scientific and Engineering Award: camera technology**)**

SCHAUSPIELER
ACTOR

Curd Jürgens
Marianne Sägebrecht
Sheryl Lee
Hanns Zischler
Andrea Sawatzki
Florian David Fitz
Elmar Wepper
Barbara Rudnik
Moritz Bleibtreu
Elya M'Barek
Martina Gedeck
Simon Verhoeven
Florian Simbeck
Heidi Brühl
Uschi Glas
Heinz Hoenig
Thea von Harbou
Werner Krauß
Josef Bierbichler
Maximilian Brückner
Markus Krojer
Günther Kaufmann

„Spatzl, schau wia i schau“
Hollywood in Germany

Fack ju Gustl: Bayerns Film- und Fernsehschaffende – eine Auswahl / Bavaria's film and television scene – an excerpt

Bernd Eichinger
Produzent · Autor · Regisseur
Producer · Writer · Director
1949–2011

REGISSEUR
DIRECTOR

Werner Herzog
Helmut Dietl
Marc Forster
Herbert Achternbusch
Marc Rothemund
Hans Steinbichler
Wolfgang Reitherman
Philipp Stölzl
Hans-Christian Schmid
Marcus H. Rosenmüller
Dominik Graf
Marco Kreuzpaintner
Joseph Vilsmaier
Florian Gallenberger
Oskar Roehler
Franz Xaver Bogner

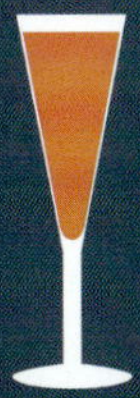

SCHAUSPIELER & REGISSEUR
ACTOR & DIRECTOR

Rainer Werner Fassbinder
Michael „Bully“ Herbig
Gerhard Polt

FERNSEHEN
TELEVISION

Horst Kummeth
Ottfried Fischer
Hans Baur
Walter Sedlmayr
Peter Steiner
Toni Berger
Gustl Bayrhammer
Karl Obermayr
Helmut Fischer
Ruth Drexel
Maxl Graf
Willy Schultes
Gisela Schneeberger
Beppo Brem
Willy Harlander
Erni Singerl
Fritz Wepper
Monika Baumgartner
Michaela May
Karl Valentin
Liesl Karlstadt
Christine Neubauer
Franz Xaver Kroetz
Gedeon Burkhard
Siegfried Rauch
Rolf Castell
Oskar Eckmüller
Max Grießer

BAVARIA FILMSTADT

Immer der Nase nach
Just follow your nose

Danke, Franke: Moderator Thomas Gottschalk hat viel geleistet für das deutsche Fernsehen. Mode-Experten meinen: zu viel. / Thanks, Frank: Moderator Thomas Gottschalk has done a great deal for German television. Fashion experts sometimes think a bit too much.

Augsburg (5x)
Häufigster bayerischer Austragungsort
Most frequent Bavarian broadcasting location

73 Minuten / minutes
überzog Gottschalk seine Sendung (8.12.1996).
longest time Gottschalk exceeded his time slot (8.12.1996).

200.000 €
Gage pro Sendung
Fee per show

Michael Mittermeier (6x)
Häufigster bayerischer Künstler auf der Bühne
Most frequent Bavarian artist on the stage

Michael „Bully" Herbig (6x)
Häufigster bayerischer Wettpate auf der Couch
Most frequent Bavarian bet sponsor on the couch

Im Guinness Buch der Rekorde für die längste Zusammenarbeit zwischen einer Marke und einem Werbeträger (Haribo, seit 1991)
Made the Guinness Book of World Records for the longest collaboration between a brand and a celebrity endorser (Haribo, since 1991)

> 25
Auszeichnungen
awards

> 25
Auftritte in Filmen und Serien
appearances in films and series

85–130 Mio. / mil. **€**
Vermögen (geschätzt)
Personal wealth (estimated)

Werk (Auswahl, jeweils höchste Einschaltquoten) / Shows (selected, with highest viewer numbers)

Zuschauer / Viewers

Show	Sender	Zuschauer / Viewers
Wetten, dass..? (1987–1992)	ZDF	**21 Mio.** / mil.
Gottschalk Late Night (1992–1995)	RTL	**4 Mio.** / mil.
Gottschalks Hausparty (1995–1997)	Sat1	**6,5 Mio.** / mil.
Wetten, dass..? (1994–2011)	ZDF	**18 Mio.** / mil.
Gottschalk America (2004)	ZDF	**2,5 Mio.** / mil.
Gottschalk zieht ein (2004)	ZDF	**3,45 Mio.** / mil.
Die Cleversten – Der große Drei-Länder-Check (2005–2006)	ZDF	**6 Mio.** / mil.
Menschen (2009–2010)	ZDF	**6,1 Mio.** / mil.
Gottschalk Live (2011–2012)	ARD	**4 Mio.** / mil.
Das Supertalent (als Juror) (2012)	RTL	**6,3 Mio.** / mil.
Die 2 – Gottschalk & Jauch gegen ALLE (seit/from 2013)	RTL	**6,8 Mio.** / mil.
Back to School (seit/from 2014)	RTL	**3,7 Mio.** / mil.

Leben / Life

*** 18.05.1950 in Bamberg**
Ministrant und Schüler in Kulmbach
Altar boy and pupil in Kulmbach

1971
Abitur, danach Lehramts-Studium (Germanistik und Geschichte) in München
University-entrance qualification, then teaching studies (German language & literature and history) in Munich

ab / from **1971**
Mitarbeiter beim BR Radio
Employed by BR Radio

1976
Wechsel ins Fernsehen
Switches to television
Thea
später / later

1982–1987
Durchbruch mit „Na Sowas!“
Breakthrough with “Na Sowas!”

1990
Umzug vom Ammersee nach Malibu
Moves from Ammersee to Malibu

2001
Bayerischer Verdienstorden
Bavarian Order of Merit

2004–2012
Besitzer von Schloss Marienfels, Remagen
Owner of Marienfels Castle, Remagen

Einmal Wagner, immer Wagner

Once Wagner, always Wagner

Die Festspiele in Bayreuth sind jedes Jahr ein großes Schaulaufen der Prominenz. Nebenbei läuft noch Musik: die zehn letzten Opern Richard Wagners / The festival in Bayreuth is THE place for European celebrities to see and be seen each year. And then there's the music of course: Richard Wagner's last ten completed operas.

29.04.1872
1. Spatenstich Festspielgebäude
Ground-breaking for festival building

13.08.1876
Beginn der ersten Festspiele
First festival commences

1.937
Sitzplätze
seats

730 m²
Hauptbühne
main stage

10–320 €
Eintrittskarte
Ticket price

30
Vorstellungen pro Jahr
performances per year

Richard Wagner
*** 22.05.1813**
in Leipzig
† 13.02.1883
in Venedig / Venice

140 m²
Orchestergraben
orchestra pit

110
Musiker
musicians

DER KANZLERIN NEUE KLEIDER / THE CHANCELLOR'S NEW CLOTHES

TUNG DER FESTSPIELE / FESTIVAL DIRECTORS

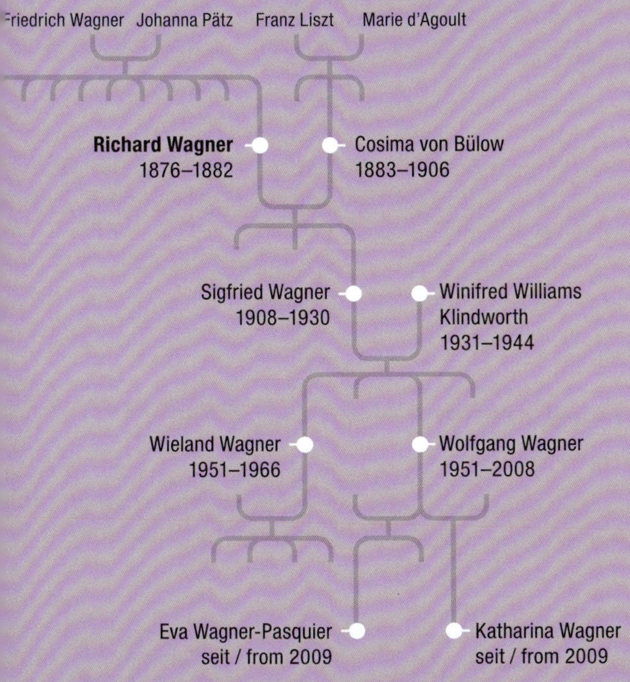

FINANZIERUNG / FINANCING

BAYREUTH-TICKETPREISE UND DEREN DURCHSCHNITTLICHE ENDPREISE BEIM WEITERVERKAUF AUF eBAY / BAYREUTH TICKET PRICES AND AVERAGE RESALE PRICES ON eBAY

Spielplan / Programme

Der fliegende Holländer
The Flying Dutchman
...
Tannhäuser
...
Lohengrin
...
Der Ring des Nibelungen (Das Rheingold, Die Walküre, Siegfried, Götterdämmerung)
The Ring of the Nibelung (The Rhine Gold, The Valkyrie, Siegfried, Twilight of the Gods)
...
Tristan und Isolde
...
Die Meistersinger von Nürnberg
The Master-Singers of Nuremberg
...
Parsifal
...
9. Sinfonie (Beethoven)
Symphony No. 9 (Beethoven)

Stammgast Angela Merkel kommt jedesmal in einer anderen Robe. Fast jedesmal.
Regular festival guest Angela Merkel dons a new gown every time. Or almost every time.

Die wollen nur spielen
They only want to play

Was für ein Theater: Bayerns Bühnen / What a drama: Bavaria's stages

ZAHL DER AUFFÜHRUNGEN AN BAYERISCHEN THEATERN (2011/2012, OHNE AMATEURE)
NUMBER OF PERFORMANCES IN BAVARIAN THEATRES (2011/2012, NOT INCL. AMATEURS)

	auf Bühnen / on stages	bei Fest- und Freilichtspielen / at festivals and open-air events	in Puppentheatern / in puppet theatres
SCHAUSPIELE / PLAYS	6.972	1.039	1.274
OPERN / OPERAS	803	74	50
OPERETTEN, MUSICALS, SINGSPIELE / OPERETTAS, MUSICALS, LIGHT OPERAS	842	96	25

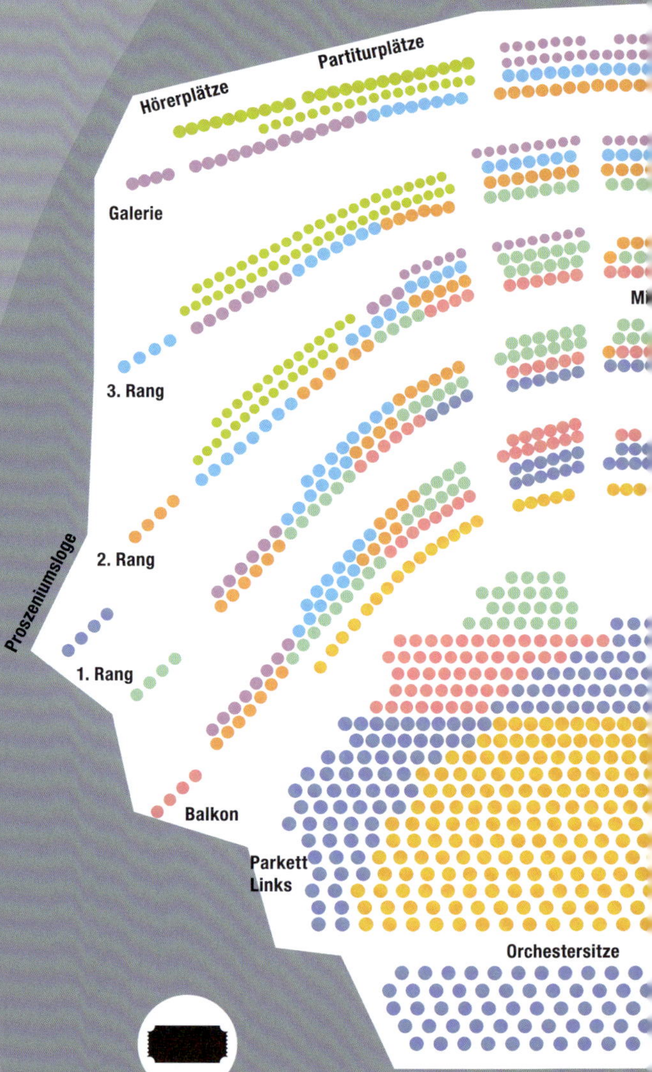

BÜHNENPRÄSENZ
STAGE PRESENCE

4 staatliche Theater in Bayern / state theatres in Bavaria

Staatstheater am Gärtnerplatz

Staatstheater Nürnberg

Bayerisches Staatsschauspiel München

Bayerische Staatsoper München

16 kommunale Theater
community theatres

30 private Bühnen
private stages

Mehr als / More Than **600 Amateurtheater**
amateur theatres

PREIS PRO SITZPLATZ (JE NACH AUFFÜHRUNG)
PRICE PER SEAT (DEPENDING ON PERFORMANCE)

- 30–264 €
- 27–230 €
- 23–190 €
- 18–148 €
- 15–104 €
- 10–69 €
- 7–28 €
- 4–20 €

DAS VORHÄNGE-SCHLOSS: DIE BAYERISCHE STAATSOPER MÜNCHEN
THE SHOWPIECE: THE BAVARIAN STATE OPERA, MUNICH

„Bayerischer Staatsoper" ist das Ensemble, „Nationaltheater" die Hauptspielstätte: Das 1818 eröffnete Gebäude am Max-Joseph-Platz ist heute das größte Opernhaus Deutschlands. / "Bayerische Staatsoper" is the ensemble, "Nationaltheater" is the venue: the building on Max Joseph Platz (opened 1818) is Germany's biggest opera house.

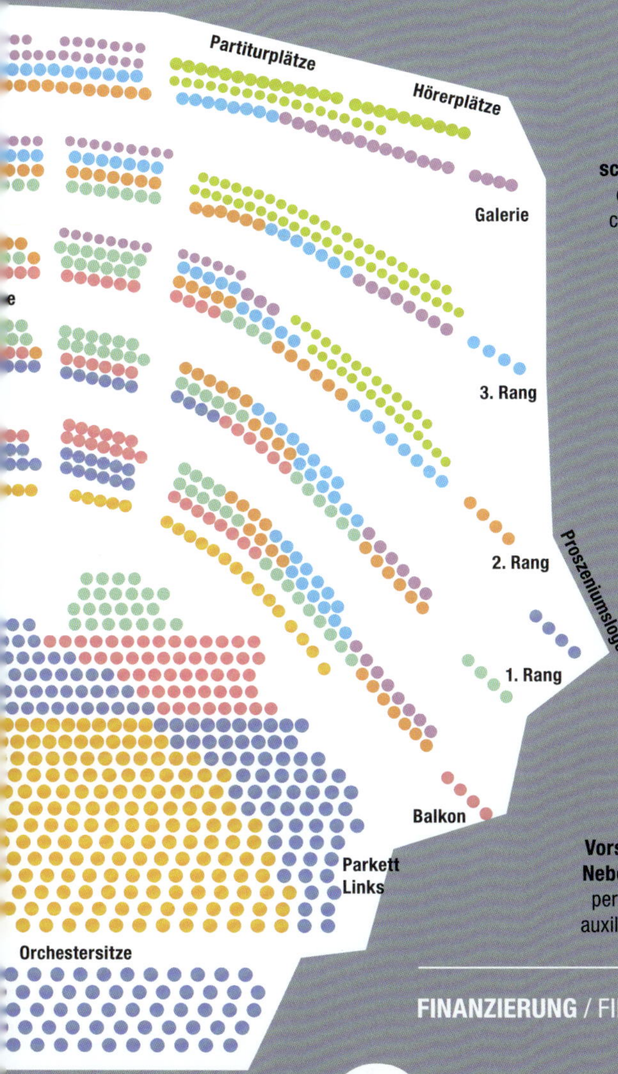

2.101
Plätze
seats

5
Extraplätze für Theaterarzt und Sanitäter
extra seats for the theatre physician and paramedics

70.000
Kristallteilchen im 3,8 t schweren Lüster (Zuschauerraum)
crystal elements in the 3.8-tonne chandelier (hanging over the house)

1,6 m²
Kleinster Arbeitsplatz: Souffleur-Kasten
Smallest workspace: prompter's box

2.500 m²
Bühne
Stage

955
Angestellte
employees

256
Vorstellungen im Nationaltheater
performances in the National Theatre

30.000
Kostüme im Fundus
costumes in the wardrobe room

446
Vorstellungen, inkl. Nebenbühnen (2013)
performances, incl. auxiliary stages (2013)

539.827
Besucher pro Jahr, inkl. Nebenbühnen
visitors per year, incl. auxiliary stages

95,2 %
Auslastung insgesamt
Total utilisation

FINANZIERUNG / FINANCING

114,57 €
Zuschuss pro Besucher
Public subsidy per visitor

99,3 Mio. / mil. € (2013)
Ausgaben / expenses

65,1 %
Zuschüsse
Subsidies

0,6 %
Mieten, Pachten und Medienerträge
Rental and leasing income and media revenues

1,7 %
Nebeneinnahmen
Supplementary income

27,6 %
Eintrittsgelder
Admission

4,1 %
Spenden, Sponsorenbeiträge
Donations, contributions from sponsors

0,9 %
Gastspiele, Kooperationen
Guest performances, cooperations

Gehst du her do!
You – get over here!

Kein schöner Land: Bayern als Urlaubsziel /
No land more lovely: Bavaria as holiday destination

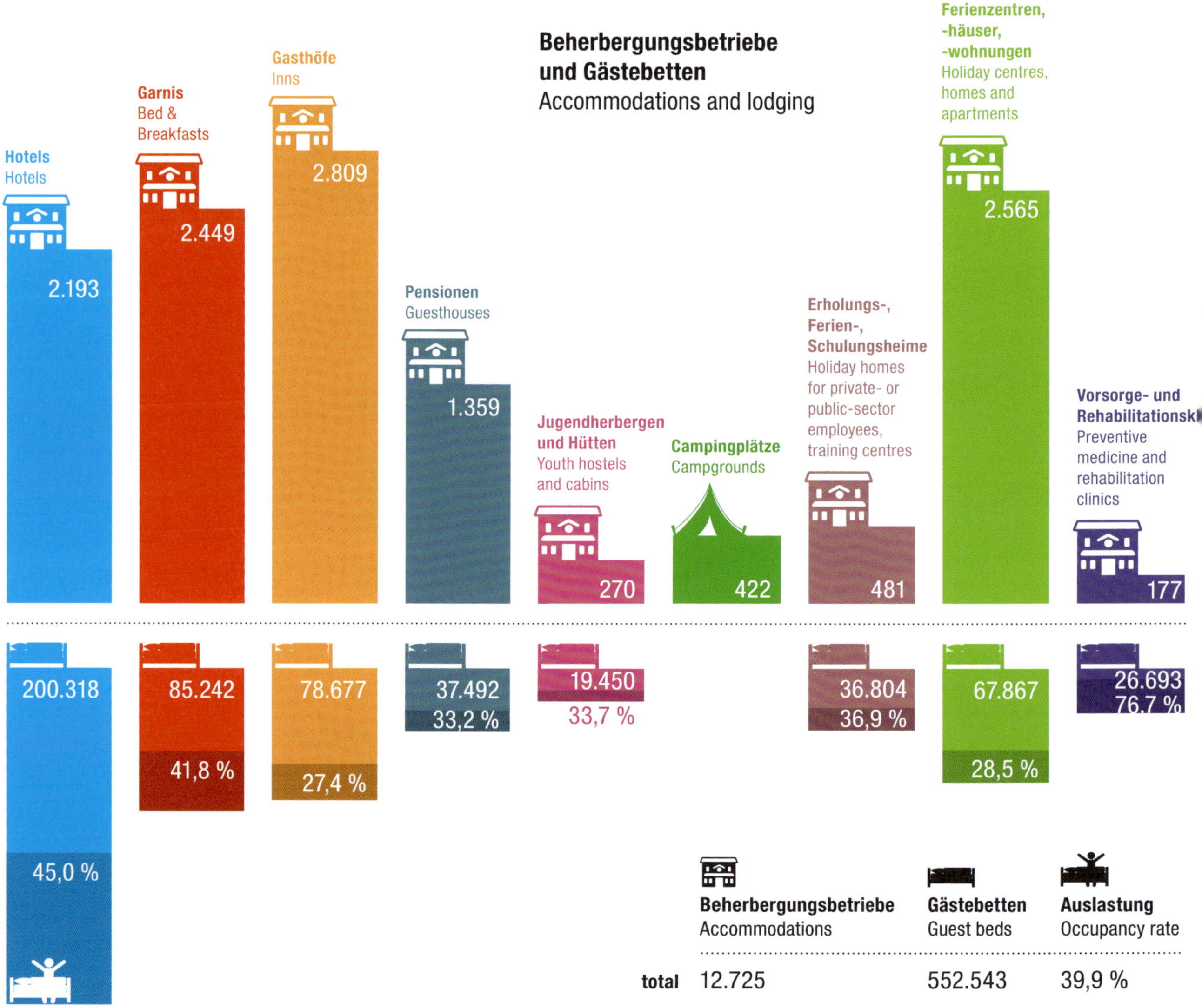

31,1 Mio. / mil.
Ankünfte pro Jahr /
arrivals per year

76,6 %
Inländer
Germans

23,4 %
Ausländer
foreigners

84 Mio. / mil.
Nächtigungen pro Jahr
overnight stays per year

2,7
Tage / days
bleibt ein Tourist durchschnittlich im Land.
a tourist stays on average in the country

Die beliebtesten Wagenburgen
The most popular car meccas (2013)

BMW-Welt
2,93 Mio. / mil. **Besucher** / visit

BMW-Museum
560.000 Besucher / visitors

Audi-Forum
400.000 Besucher / visitors

nzahl Touristen nach Regierungsbezirk pro Jahr
umber of tourists per administrative district per year

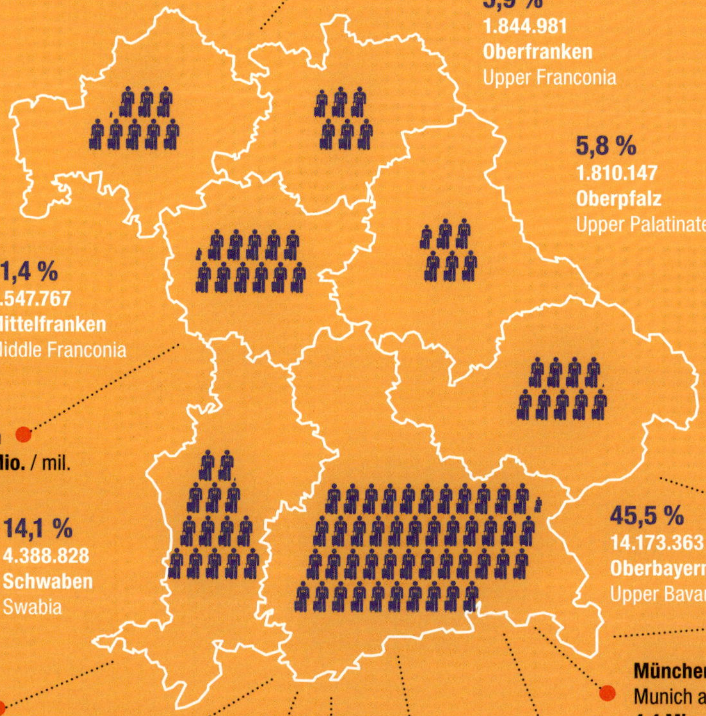

o die Bayern-Urlauber herkommen
here tourists in Bavaria come from

76,6 % **Deutschland** Germany

2,4 % **Niederlande** Netherlands

2,1 % **Österreich** Austria

2,1 % **USA**

1,9 % **Italien** Italy

1,7 % **Schweiz** Switzerland

1,5 % **Vereinigtes Königreich** United Kingdom

0,9 % **Russland** Russia

0,9 % **Japan**

ie beliebtesten ehenswürdigkeiten
he most popular ttractions **(2012)**

1.402.717 **Schloss Neuschwanstein** Neuschwanstein Castle

509.194 **Schlossanlage Nymphenburg** Nymphenburg Palace

436.968 **Schloss Linderhof** Linderhof Palace

411.300 **Schloss Herrenchiemsee** Herrenchiemsee Palace

339.243 **Residenz Würzburg** Würzburg Residence

Im Auftrag Ihrer Majestät
By order of Your Majesty

König Ludwig II. hat nicht nur luxuriös gewohnt, sondern auch herrschaftlich bauen lassen. Nicht umsonst heißt der Kerl „Märchenkönig". / King Ludwig II not only lived in the lap of luxury — he also commissioned the building of a series of opulent residences, earning him the nickname "The Fairytale King".

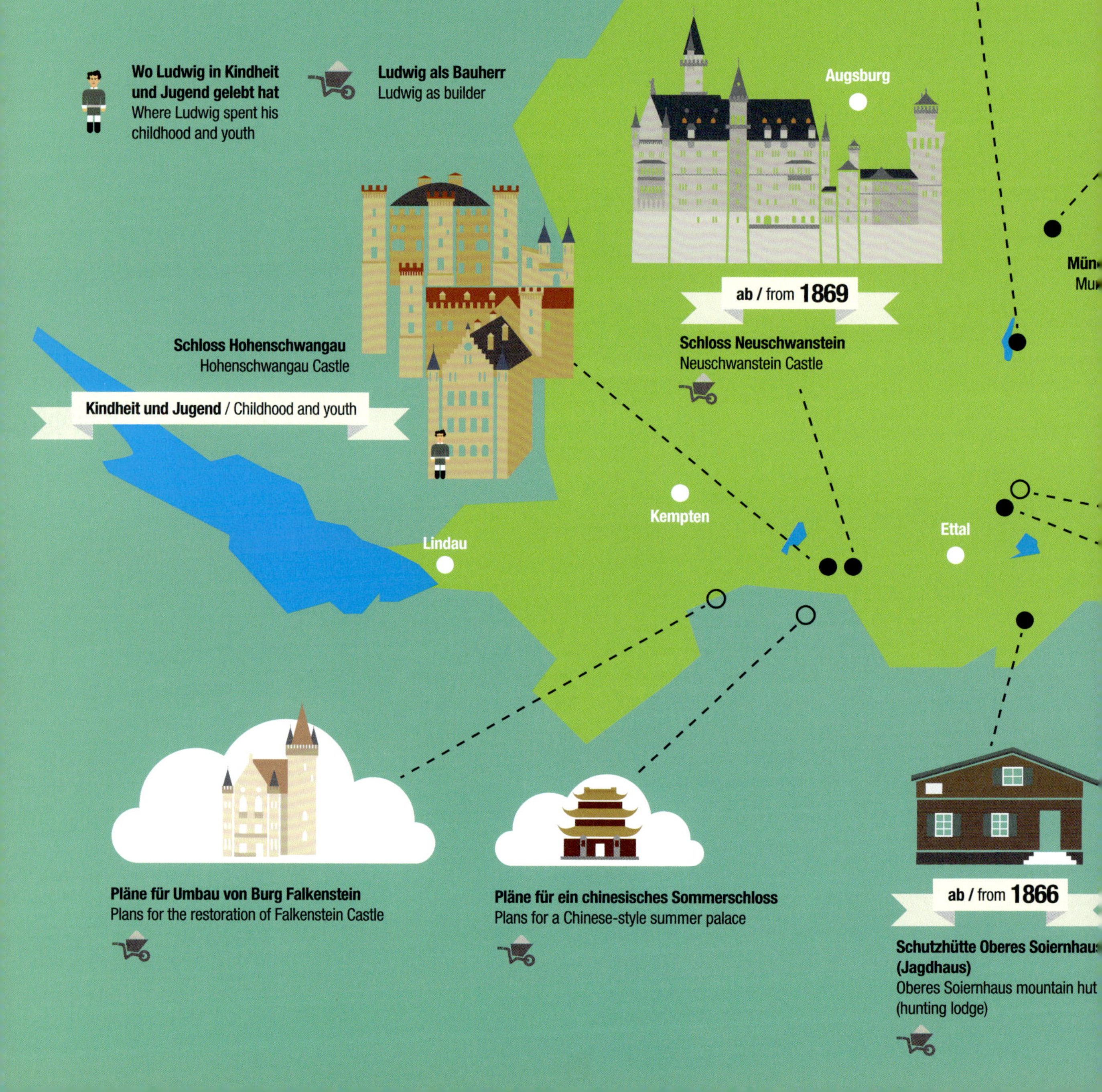

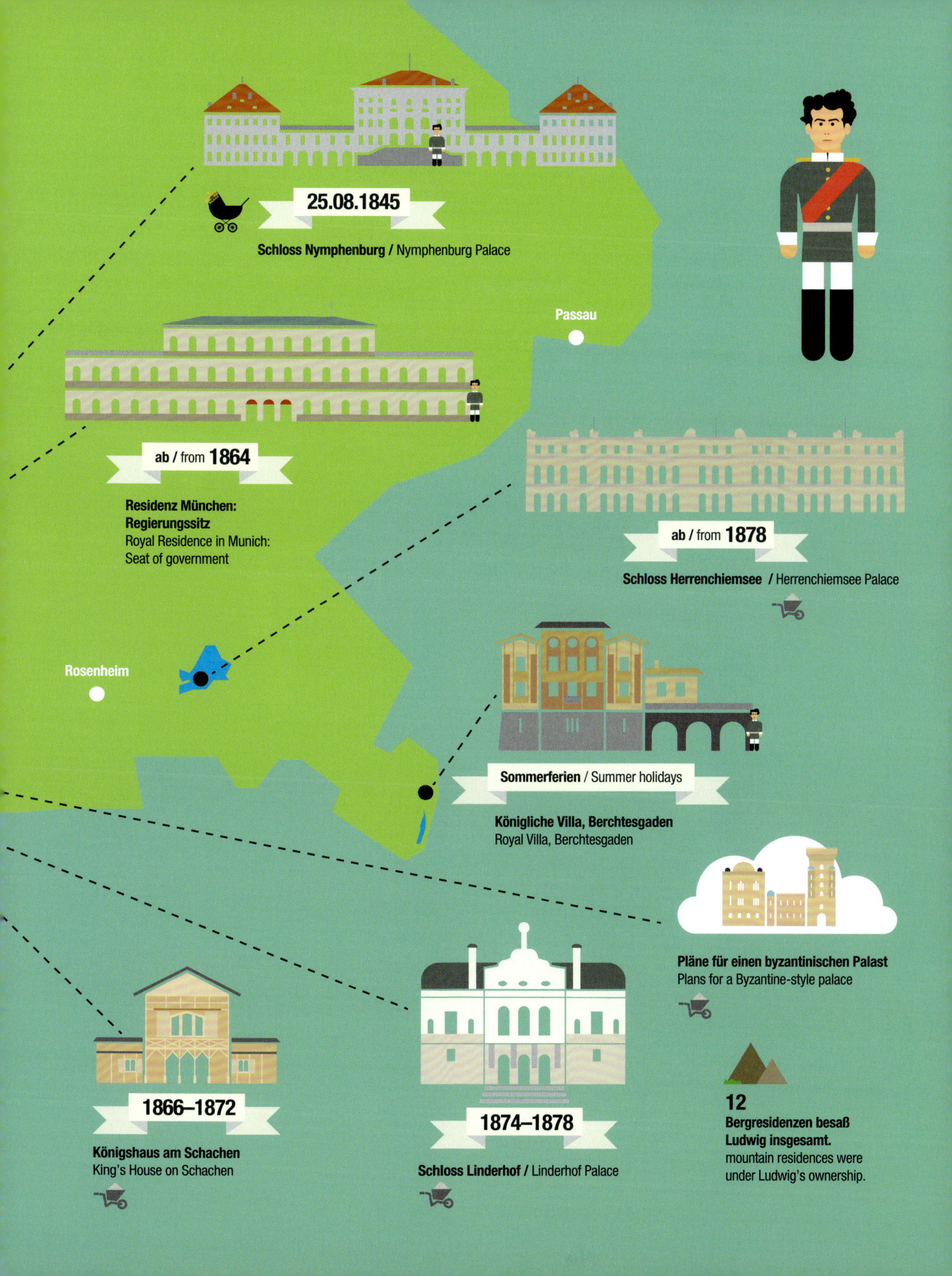
25.08.1845
Schloss Nymphenburg / Nymphenburg Palace
Passau
ab / from 1864
Residenz München: Regierungssitz
Royal Residence in Munich: Seat of government
ab / from 1878
Schloss Herrenchiemsee / Herrenchiemsee Palace
Rosenheim
Sommerferien / Summer holidays
Königliche Villa, Berchtesgaden
Royal Villa, Berchtesgaden
Pläne für einen byzantinischen Palast
Plans for a Byzantine-style palace
1866–1872
Königshaus am Schachen
King's House on Schachen
1874–1878
Schloss Linderhof / Linderhof Palace
12
Bergresidenzen besaß Ludwig insgesamt.
mountain residences were under Ludwig's ownership.

Königlich-kaiserlich
Royal-Imperial

Kaum jemand wird in Bayern so verehrt und verklärt wie Ludwig II. Einzig Fußballkaiser Franz Beckenbauer kommt an die Popularität des Märchenkönigs heran. Dabei könnten ihre Lebensläufe, die genau ein Jahrhundert trennen, nicht unterschiedlicher sein. Ein aristokratischer Vergleich. / King Ludwig II is venerated and glorified in Bavaria like hardly any other figure. Only the "emperor" of football, Franz Beckenbauer, comes close to matching the fairytale king's popularity. And yet the two men's biographies, separated by exactly one century, could hardly be more different. An aristocratic comparison.

FRANZ ANTON BECKENBAUER

Kaiser im 20. Jahrhundert
Emperor in the 20th century

Eltern / Parents: **Postobersekretär Franz sen. & Antonie (geb. Hupfauf)**
Postal worker Franz sen. & Antonie (née Hupfauf)

1945
München Giesing

Jugend / Youth: **SC 1906 München**

Thomas

1. Spiel für den FC Bayern
1st match played for FC Bayern

1. Werbevertrag (Knorr Fertigsuppen)
1st advertising contract (Knorr instant soups)

1. von 4 DFB-Pokalen
1st of 4 DFB (German Football Association) Cups

Brigitte Wittmann

Michael

Spitzname „Der Kaiser"
Nickname "The Emperor"

Stefan

1. von 5 Deutsche Meistersch
1st of 5 Gern Championsh titles

`45 · `61 · `62 · `63 · `64 · `66 · `67 · `68

LUDWIG II

König im 19. Jahrhundert
King in the 19th century

1845
Schloss Nymphenburg
Nymphenburg Palace

Eltern / Parents: Kronprinz Maximilian & Kronprinzessin Marie
Crown Prince Maximilian & Crown Princess Marie

Jugend / Youth: **Schloss Hohenschwangau**
Hohenschwangau Palace

Sieht Richard Wagners Opern
Sees Richard Wagner's operas

Beginnt Studium an der Münchner Universität: Physik, Chemie, Logik und Geschichte der Philosophie
Begins studies at Munich University: physics, chemistry, logic and history of philosophy

† König Maximilian: Ludwig wird König von Bayern
† King Maximilian: Ludwig becomes King of Bavaria

Trifft / Meets **Richard Wagner.**

Schickt Bayern an der Seite Österreichs in den Deutschen Krieg – und verliert.
Sends Bavaria to war on Austria's side – and is defeated.

Verlobung mit Sophie, der Schwester von Kaiserin Sisi. Später Entlobung.
Engaged to Sophie, sister of Empress Sisi. Later broken off.

Gründet heutige *Technische Universität München.*
Founds today's *Technische Universität München.*

2006 · 2004 · 2003 · 2000 · '91 · '90

Heidi Burmester

Bis heute kaiserliche Lichtgestalt
Still today an imperial shining light

Scheidung von Sybille
Divorce from Sybille

Francesca mit / with **Heidi**

Joel Maximilian mit / with **Heidi Burmester (FC-Bayern-München-Sekretärin** / secretary**)**

Technischer Direktor bei Olympique Marseille; französischer Meister
Technical director of Olympique Marseille; French champion

Sybille Weimar (ehemalige DFB-Sekretärin
former German Football Association secretary**)**

Weltmeister als Teamchef: Beckenbauer wird zu Lichtgestalt
World champion as team chief: Beckenbauer becomes a leading light

WM-Botschafter für die deutsche Bewerbung um die Austragung des Turniers 2006.
World Cup ambassador for Germany's bid to host the tournament in 2006.

Vizepräsident beim FCB, später Präsident und Ehrenpräsident
Vice-president of FC Bayern München, later president, then honorary president

Vize-Weltmeister als Teamchef
Team is runner-up in FIFA World Cup

Ärger mit der Steuer: zahlt 1,8 Mio DM (ca. 920.000 €) nach
Tax trouble: has to pay 1.8 mil. DM (ca. € 920,000) in back taxes

Rückkehr nach Deutschland, Spieler beim HSV
Returns to Germany, plays for HSV in Hamburg

Kurze Rückkehr zu New York Cosmos, endgültiges Karriereende
Briefly returns to the New York Cosmos, final end of career as player

ropameister und ropas Fußballer s Jahres
FA European ampionship d European otballer of the Year

Weltmeister
FIFA World Cup
1. von 3 Europapokalen der Landesmeister
1st of 3 UEFA Champions League Cups

Weltpokalsieger
Intercontinental Cup

Umzug nach New York, Spieler bei Cosmos
Moves to New York, plays for the Cosmos

Karriereende in Deutschland
Ends career as player in Germany

Teamchef der Deutschen Nationalmannschaft
Team coach of German National Football Team

'70 · '72 · '74 · '76 · '77 · '78 · '80 · '82 · '83 · '84 · '86

kt Armee in den eichen sch-Französischen . Bayern wird es neuen Deutschen es unter dem utschen Kaiser lm I.
army to victory Franco-German War. ia becomes part of w German Reich the first German Emperor, m I.

Baubeginn Schloss Linderhof
Building begins on Linderhof Palace

Baubeginn Schloss Herrenchiemsee
Building begins on Herrenchiemsee Palace

Wird durch Regierung entmündigt und nach Schloss Berg am Starnberger See gebracht. Ertrinkt am 13. Juni im See unter mysteriösen Umständen.
Deposed by the government and brought to Berg Castle on Lake Starnberg. Drowns in the lake on 13 June under mysterious circumstances.

Seither als Kini königliche Lichtgestalt
Since then remembered as *Kini, "Our Cherished King"*.

Letzter öffentlicher Auftritt vor der Generalprobe der Bayreuther Festspiele
Last public appearance at a dress rehearsal for the Bayreuth Festival

Baubeginn Schloss Neuschwanstein
Building begins on Neuschwanstein Castle

Stern des Südens

Star of the South

Viel Feind', viel Ehr': Seit 50 Jahren dominiert der FC Bayern die Bundesliga – vor allem dank Uli Hoeneß. /
No guts, no glory: For 50 years FC Bayern has dominated the National League – thanks especially to Uli Hoene

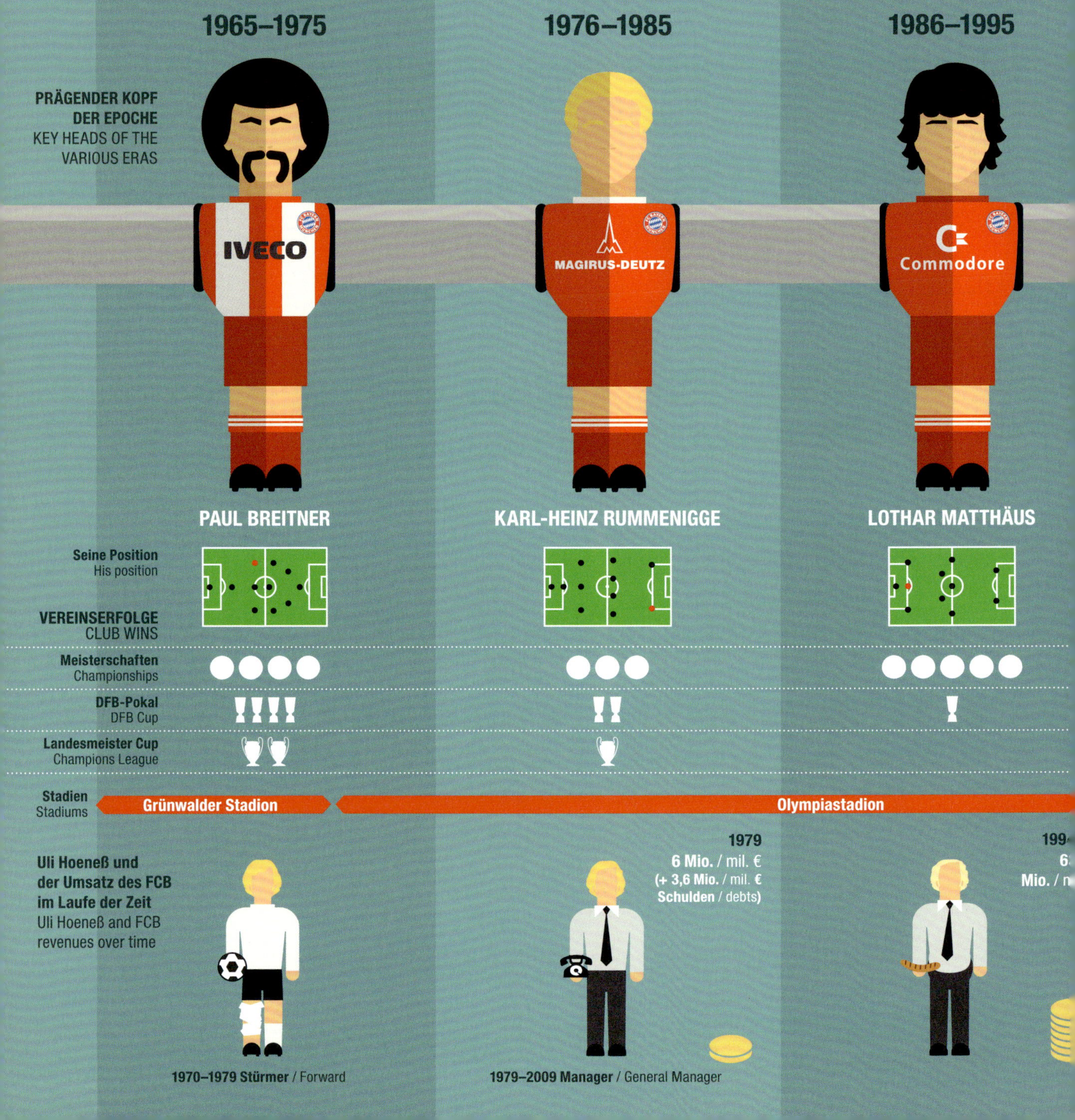

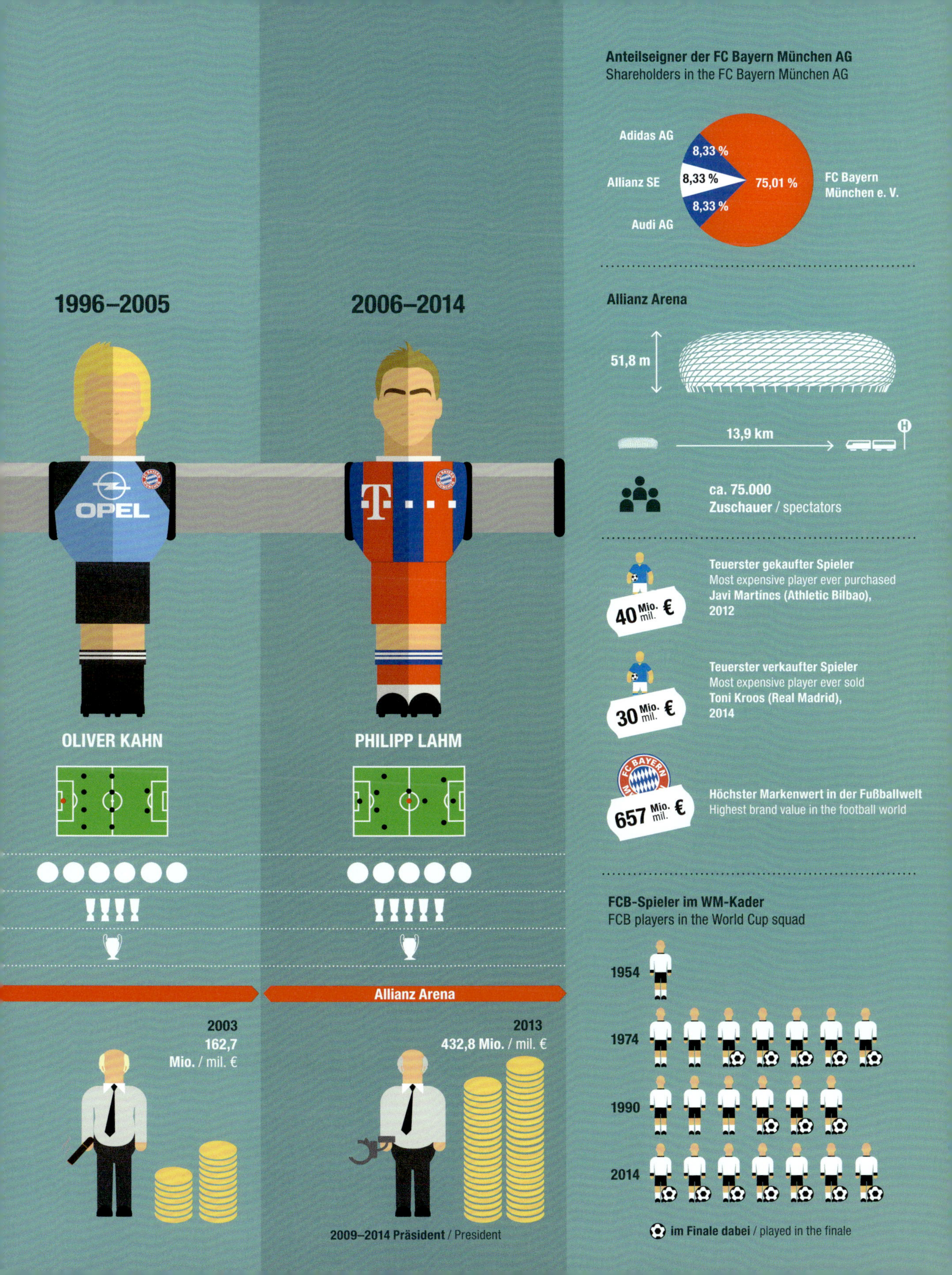
1996–2005
2006–2014
OPEL
T
OLIVER KAHN
PHILIPP LAHM
Allianz Arena
2003
162,7
Mio. / mil. €
2013
432,8 Mio. / mil. €
2009–2014 Präsident / President
Anteilseigner der FC Bayern München AG
Shareholders in the FC Bayern München AG
Adidas AG
8,33 %
Allianz SE
8,33 %
Audi AG
8,33 %
75,01 %
FC Bayern München e. V.
Allianz Arena
51,8 m
13,9 km
ca. 75.000
Zuschauer / spectators
Teuerster gekaufter Spieler
Most expensive player ever purchased
Javi Martines (Athletic Bilbao),
2012
40 Mio. mil. €
Teuerster verkaufter Spieler
Most expensive player ever sold
Toni Kroos (Real Madrid),
2014
30 Mio. mil. €
FC BAYERN
657 Mio. mil. €
Höchster Markenwert in der Fußballwelt
Highest brand value in the football world
FCB-Spieler im WM-Kader
FCB players in the World Cup squad
1954
1974
1990
2014
im Finale dabei / played in the finale

„Geht's raus und spielt's Fußball"

"Go out there and play ball!"

Beckenbauers Wort ist Gesetz: Die bayerischen Kicker sind stets rekordverdächtig. Auch ohne den FCB / Beckenbauer's word is law: Bavaria has some record-breaking kickers. Even without FC Bayern.

Weiß-blaues Fußballfieber
White-and-blue football fever

29.135
Mannschaften / teams

16.000
Schiedsrichter / referees

1.530.842
Vereinsmitglieder
club members

263.482
Buben
boys

129.999
junge Männer (15–18)
young men (15–18)

70.042
Mädchen (bis 16)
girls (16 and under)

151.041
Frauen
women

916.278
Männer
men

BFV

4.682
Vereine beim größten Landesverband des Deutschen Fußball-Bunds, dem Bayerischen Fußball-Verband /
clubs in the biggest regional association in the German Football Association: the Bavarian Football Association

Bayerische Klubs in der Bundesliga (ohne FCB) / Bavarian clubs in the National League (without FCB)

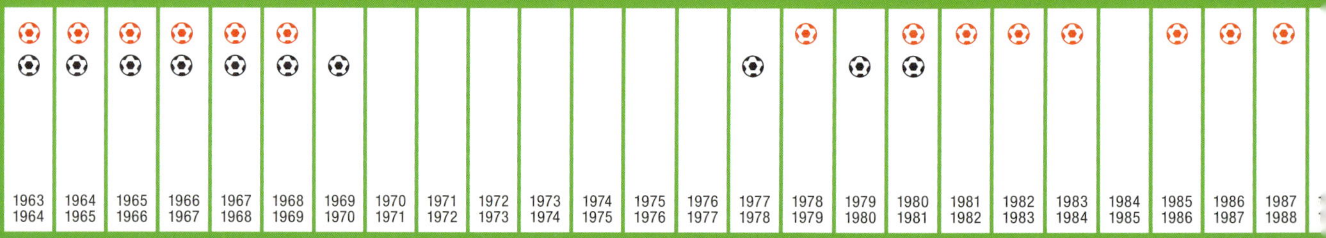

Deutsche Rekorde aus dem FCB-freien Bayern
German records from FCB-free Bavaria

Kleinster Bundesligist aller Zeiten
Smallest club in the league of all time
Unterhaching
(22.000 Einwohner / inhabitants**)**

Beliebtester Fußball-Hit
Most popular football hit
'54, '74, '90, 2006
vom Album
„You Have to Win Zweikampf"
der Sportfreunde Stiller
from the album
"You Have to Win Zweikampf"
by Sportfreunde Stiller

Die meisten Deutschen Meisterschaften vor Einführung der Bundesliga 1965
The most German Championships before the introduction of the National League in 1965
8 (1. FC Nürnberg)

Inoffizieller Zuschauerrekord in der 2. Bundesliga
Inofficial audience record in the Second League
ca. 90.000 (1973)
(in Augsburg gegen den TSV 1860 München / in Augsburg against TSV 1860 München**)**

Mächtigstes Ehrenmitglied
Most powerful honorary member
Henry Kissinger
(SpVgg Greuther Fürth)

Die meisten Bundesliga-Aufstiege
The most promotions in the league tables
7 (1. FC Nürnberg)

Offizieller Zuschauerrekord in der 2. Bundesliga
Official audience record in the Second League
77.116 (2011)
(in Augsburg gegen Hertha BSC / in Augsburg against Hertha BSC**)**

Größte Elfmeter-Killer
Biggest penalty shoot-out killers
Simon Jentzsch
Thomas Zander
beide 1860 (jeweils 7 hintereinander verschossene Elfer gegen sie)
both in 1860 (each blocked 7 shoot-out kicks in a row)

Die meisten Bundesliga-Abstiege
The most demotions in the league tables
8 (1. FC Nürnberg)

Durstigster Moderator
Thirstiest moderator
Waldemar Hartmann
(Laut Rudi Völler: „Drei Weizenbier" auf Sendung / According to Rudi Völler: "Three wheat beers" while on the air)

Lustigste Spieler
Funniest players
Monthy Python
(Das „Fußballspiel der Philosophen" haben die Briten im 60er-Stadion gedreht.)
(The British comedy troupe shot the "Philosophers' Football Match" at the 60er (Grünwald) Stadium.)

Unter Brüdern
Between brothers

Adidas und Puma gehören heute hinter Nike zu den größten internationalen Sportartikelherstellern. Sie sind erbitterte Konkurrenten auf dem Weltmarkt – dabei entstammen beide Konzerne einem Familienunternehmen aus der fränkischen Kleinstadt Herzogenaurach. / Today, Adidas and Puma are amongst the biggest international sportswear makers, second only to Nike. The two corporate groups are bitter rivals on the world market – and yet both stem from the same family-run business in the small Franconian town of Herzogenaurach.

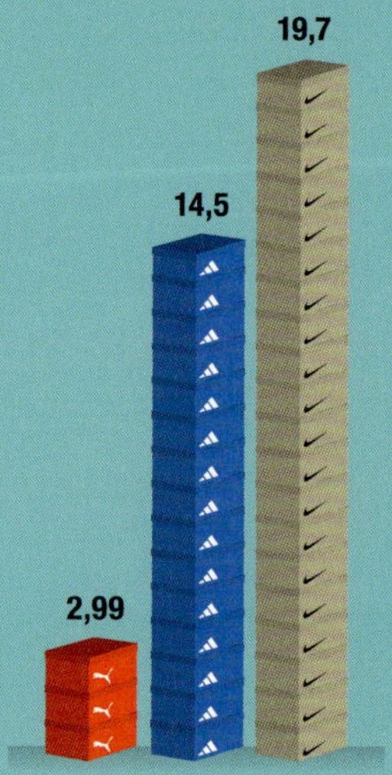

Umsatz / Turnover **2013 in Mrd. / bn**

Ausrüster der Nationalmannschaften bei der FIFA-WM 2014 in Brasilien
Outfitters of the national teams at the FIFA World Cup 2014 in Brazil

Puma

- Italien / Italy
- Schweiz / Switzerland
- Uruguay
- Chile
- Elfenbeinküste / Ivory Coast
- Ghana
- Kamerun / Cameroon
- Algerien / Algeria

Adidas

- Deutschland / Germany
- Argentinien / Argentina
- Japan
- Kolumbien / Columbia
- Russland / Russia
- Spanien / Spain
- Mexiko / Mexico
- Nigeria
- Bosnien-Herzegowina / Bosnia-Herzegovina

FIFA WORLD CUP Brasil

Nike

- Brasilien / Brazil
- Südkorea / South Korea
- Niederlande / Netherlands
- USA
- England
- Griechenland / Greece
- Portugal
- Frankreich / France
- Kroatien / Croatia
- Australien / Australia

andere / others

- Iran
- Costa Rica
- Belgien / Belgium
- Ecuador
- Honduras

Mitarbeiter / Employees 2013
10.982
50.728
48.000
1989
kommen verkaufen ihre Puma-Anteile
Descendants sell their Puma shares.
1990
Nachkommen verkaufen Ihre Adidas-Anteile
Descendants sell their Adidas shares.
1978
Adi
Rudolf
1974
PUMA
adidas
Firma wird aufgeteilt.
The company splits up.
1949
ADOLF DASSLER adidas SPORTSCHUHE
Adidas (Kurzform von / short for Adi Dassler)
1948
Rudolfs Familie zieht aus dem gemeinsamen Haus aus.
Rudolf's family moves out of the shared homestead.
RUDOLF DASSLER PUMA SCHUHFABRIK
2. Weltkrieg
Rudolf wird eingezogen.
World War II
Rudolf is drafted.
1943
Adi leitet zuhause das Unternehmen.
Adi runs the company back home.
NSDAP
Dassler-Brüder, beide in der NSDAP, profitieren von Hitlers Nachfrage.
Both Dassler brothers are in the Nazi Party and profit from the high demand under Hitler.
Frauen verstehen sich nicht, Familien entfremden sich.
The wives don't get along and the families become estranged.
1934
Adi
Käthe
Rudolf
Friedl
1928
Erste Dassler-Schuhe bei Olympia in Amsterdam
First Dassler shoes at the Olympics, in Amsterdam
1924
DASSLER
Söhne Adolf und Rudolf gründen „Gebrüder Dassler Schuhfabrik"
Sons Adolf and Rudolf found the "Dassler Brothers Shoe Factory".
Christoph & Paulina Dassler, Herzogenaurach

So sehen Siegerinnen aus
Women on the winner's rostrum

Deutschland liebt seine starken Sportler – doch wenn es ernst wird, versagen die männlichen Wettkämpfer oft reihenweise. Zum Glück gibt es da noch die Athletinnen aus Bayern. / Germany reveres its athletes – but when the going gets tough, the male competitors often come up short. Luckily, Bavaria has produced a host of female champions.

SKI ALPIN / ALPINE SKIING

MARIA HÖFL-RIESCH

* 1984, Garmisch-Partenkirchen
Beruf: Zollbeamtin / Occupation: Customs officer

Bilanz bei den Olympischen Winterspielen 2010 & 2014
Medal count at the Winter Olympics 2010 & 2014

Bilanz der deutschen Männer im selben Zeitraum
Medal count for the German male competitors at the same games:

EISSCHNELLLAUF / SPEED SKATING

ANNI FRIESINGER-POSTMA

* 1977, Bad Reichenhall
Beruf: Designerin, Markenbotschafterin, Privatpilotin, Moderatorin / Occupation: Designer, brand ambassador, private pilot, moderator

Bilanz bei den Olympischen Winterspielen 1998–2010
Medal count at the Winter Olympics 1998–2010

Bilanz der deutschen Männer im selben Zeitraum
Medal count for the German male competitors at the same games

BIATHLON

MAGDALENA NEUNER

* 1987, Garmisch-Partenkirchen
Beruf: Zollbeamtin a. D. / Occupation: Former customs officer

Bilanz bei den Olympischen Winterspielen 2010
Medal count at the Winter Olympics 2010

Bilanz der deutschen Männer im selben Zeitraum
Medal count for the German male competitors at the same games

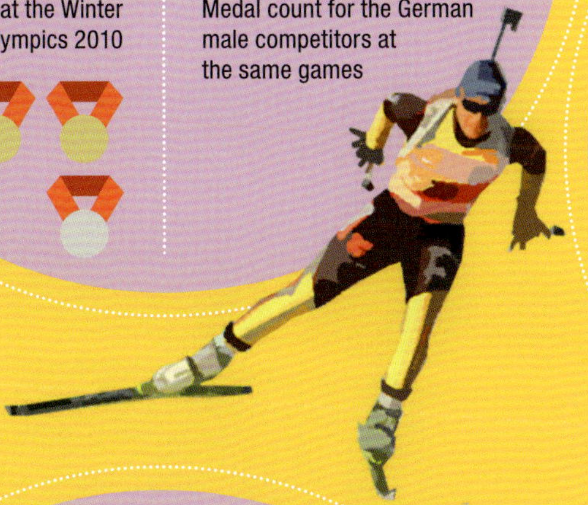

KICKBOXEN / KICKBOXING

CHRISTINE THEISS

* 1980, Greiz (Thüringen), aufgewachsen in Bayreuth, lebt in München / grew up in Bavaria, lives in Munich
Beruf: Zahnärztin / Occupation: Dentist

Bilanz 2007–2013
Track record 2007–2013

Bilanz der deutschen Männer im selben Zeitraum
Track record for German male kickboxers during the same period

FUßBALL / FOOTBALL

NADINE ANGERER

* 1978, Lohr am Main
Beruf: Physiotherapeutin / Occupation: Physiotherapist

Bilanz bei Fußballturnieren seit 1997 mit der Nationalmannschaft
Track record at football tournaments since 1997 with the German National Team

UEFA UEFA UEFA UEFA UEFA
FIFA FIFA

Bilanz der deutschen Männer im selben Zeitraum
Track record for the German male team during the same period

FIFA

SKI ALPIN / ALPINE SKIING

ANNA SCHAFFELHUBER

* 1993, Regensburg
Beruf: Jura-Studentin / Occupation: Law student

Bilanz bei den Paralympics 2014
Medal count at the Paralympics 2014

Bilanz der deutschen Männer im selben Zeitraum
Medal count for the German male competitors at the same games

Wer hat's erfunden?
Who invented it?

Mehr als ein Viertel aller deutschen Patente werden im Freistaat angemeldet. Aber bereits vor Siemens und Co. veränderten Innovationen aus Bayern die Welt. / More than a quarter of all German patents originate in Bavaria. But even before Siemens and the rest came onto the scene, Bavarian innovations were changing the world.

Vorstandsvorsitzender / Chairman of the Board:
Joe Kaeser
(* 1957 als / as **Josef Käser in Arnbruck, Niederbayern** / Lower Bavaria**)**

Sitz / Headquarters
München / Munich **(& Berlin)**

DER PATENTE-KONZERN: DIE SIEMENS AG
THE PATENT FACTORY: SIEMENS AG

78 Milliarden / billion €
Umsatz / Turnover **(2011/2012)**

370.000
Mitarbeiter
Employees

„Eine wesentliche Ursache für das Aufblühen unserer Fabrikation sehe ich darin, dass die Gegenstände unserer Fabrikation zum großen Teil auf eigenen Erfindungen beruhten."
"One of the main reasons our production is flourishing is that the products we make are based in large part on our own inventions."

Werner von Siemens (1816–1892)

Größter Standort in Bayern
Largest company location in Bavaria
Erlangen (23.000 Mitarbeiter / employees**)**

SIEMENS-FORSCHUNG / RESEARCH BY SIEMENS

> 60.000
Patente
patents

35 %
davon „Grüne Patente" für nachhaltige Technologien
thereof "green patents" for sustainable technologies

18
Patentanmeldungen pro Arbeitstag
patent applications per workday

38
Erfindungen pro Arbeitstag
inventions every workday

4,3 Milliarden / billion €
Investitionen in Forschung und Entwicklung pro Jahr
Annual investment volume in research and development

13.300
Forscher und Entwickler in Deutschland
researchers and developers in Germany

16.500
in mehr als 30 anderen Ländern
in more than 30 other countries

IN BAYERN GEMACHTE ERFINDUNGEN
INVENTIONS MADE IN BAVARIA

Elfmeterschießen
Penalty shoot-out
1970 Karl Wald
(in München / Munich)

Röntgenstrahlen
X-ray
1895 Wilhelm Conrad Röntgen
(in Würzburg entdeckt /
discovered in Würzburg)

um / around **1504**
Taschenuhr
Pocket watch
Peter Henlein
(Nürnberg)

1655
Rollstuhl
Wheelchair
Stephan Farfler
(Altdorf bei / near **Nürnberg)**

1872
Jeans
Levi Strauss
(Buttenheim)

1815
Metronom
Metronome
Johann Nepomuk Mälzel
(Regensburg)

2002
„Gludernde Lot“
e of many slips of the tongue,
Edmund Stoiber (CSU)
egendärer Wortneuschöpfer /
legendary neologist)

1951
Airbag
Walter Linderer
(München / Munich)

1907
„Mensch ärgere Dich nicht“
A game similar to Ludo
Josef Friedrich Schmidt
(München / Munich)

Mitte 19. Jh.
Mid-19th century
Kneipp-Medizin und Wasserkur mit Wassertreten
Kneipp medicine and hydrotherapy, including treading water
Sebastian Anton Kneipp (Stephansried)

1982
MP3-Format
MP3 format
Karlheinz Brandenburg
(Erlangen)

1952
Skibindung
Ski bindings
Hannes Marker
(Garmisch-Partenkirchen)

1929
Tempo
Tempo-Taschentuch
Tempo paper handkerchief
Vereinigte Papierwerke
Nürnberg

VON BAYERN GEMACHTE ERFINDUNGEN
INVENTIONS MADE BY BAVARIANS

Brummbrumm
Broom broom

Die Bayern und ihre Autos – eine Liebesgeschichte / The Bavarians and their cars – a love story

> 17 Mio. / mil.
in Burghaslach gefertigte BIG-Bobby-Cars wurden schon verkauft.
BIG Bobby Cars made in Burghaslach have been sold to date.

Gesamtbestand / Total vehicles

9.103.344
Kraftfahrzeuge / vehicles

814.571
Krafträder
motorcycles

7.214.493
Personenkraftwagen
cars

13.320
Kraftomnibusse
buses

387.828
Lastkraftwagen
lorries

627.886
Zulassungspflichtige Zugmaschinen
tractors and similar

45.246
andere Kraftfahrzeuge
other vehicles

Fahrprüfung / Driving test

268.999
theoretische Prüfungen
written tests

27,8 %
nicht bestanden
failure rate

265.143
praktische Prüfungen
road tests

24,5 %
nicht bestanden
failure rate

ca. 215.000
Führerscheine werden pro Jahr ausgestellt.
driver's licences are issued each year.

Fahrzeugzulassungen
Vehicle registrations

48.962
PKWs werden durchschnittlich im Monat zugelassen.
cars are registered per month on average.

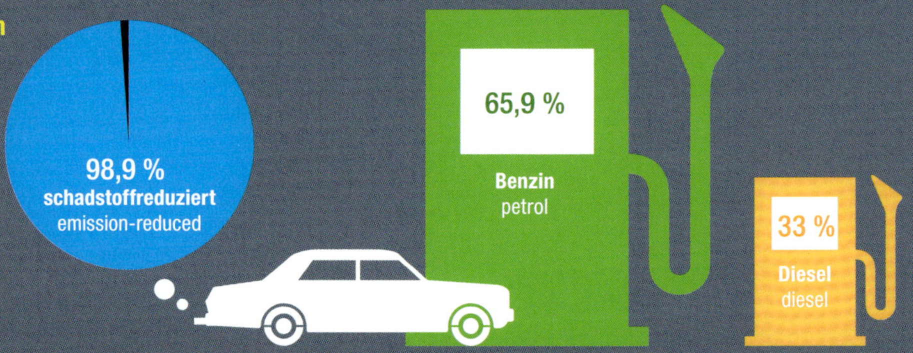

Unfälle im Straßenverkehr / Traffic accidents

364.373
Straßenverkehrsunfälle
traffic accidents

85,7 %
mit Sachschaden
with material damage

14,3 %
mit Personenschaden
with personal injury

70.143
Verunglückte
casualties

99,1 %
Verletzte
injuries

0,9 %
Getötete
fatalities

FR SA

Freitags und samstags passieren die meisten Straßenverkehrsunfälle.
Most traffic accidents occur on Friday and Saturday.

Hauptursachen für tödliche Unfälle
Main causes for fatal accidents

1. **zu hohe Geschwindigkeit**
   excessive speed
2. **Vorfahrt missachtet**
   disregarding right of way
3. **Alkohol** / alcohol

Frau am Steuer – ungeheuer?
Women drivers – a menace?

79.268
Kraftfahrzeugführer waren 2012 an gravierenden Unfällen beteiligt.
drivers were involved in serious accidents in 2012.

66,5 % 33,5 %

Diebstahl / Theft

Tankbetrug in Bayern – In welcher bayerischen Stadt wird am meisten Sprit gestohlen?
Scams at the petrol station – In which Bavarian town is the most petrol stolen?

15 Fälle pro Jahr pro Tankstelle
cases per year per petrol station

Stadt	Fälle
PASSAU	15
WÜRZBURG	9
GARMISCH-PARTENKIRCHEN	7
ASCHAFFENBURG, AUGSBURG, KEMPTEN, MÜNCHEN	6
COBURG	5
BAMBERG, ERLANGEN, INGOLSTADT, NÜMBERG, REGENSBURG, ROSENHEIM	4
BAYREUTH, HOF	3
AMBERG, FÜRTH, STRAUBING, WEIDEN	2

Meistgeklaute Autos in Deutschland
The cars most frequently stolen in Germany

BMW X6 Xdrive 40D
BMW M3 Coupé

917
Traktoren werden durchschnittlich im Monat zugelassen.
tractors are registered per month on average.

46 %
Benzin
petrol

53 %
Diesel
diesel

1 %
Hybrid, Gas, Elektro
hybrid, gas, electric

Die Herren der Ringe
The Lords of the Rings

Audi-Modelle werden weltweit verkauft – und längst auch weltweit produziert. Geschichte einer bayerischen Globalisierung / Audi models are sold worldwide – and have long been produced worldwide as well. The story of a Bavarian globalisation.

PRODUKTIONSSTÄTTEN DES AUDI-KONZERNS
AUDI-GROUP PRODUCTION SITES

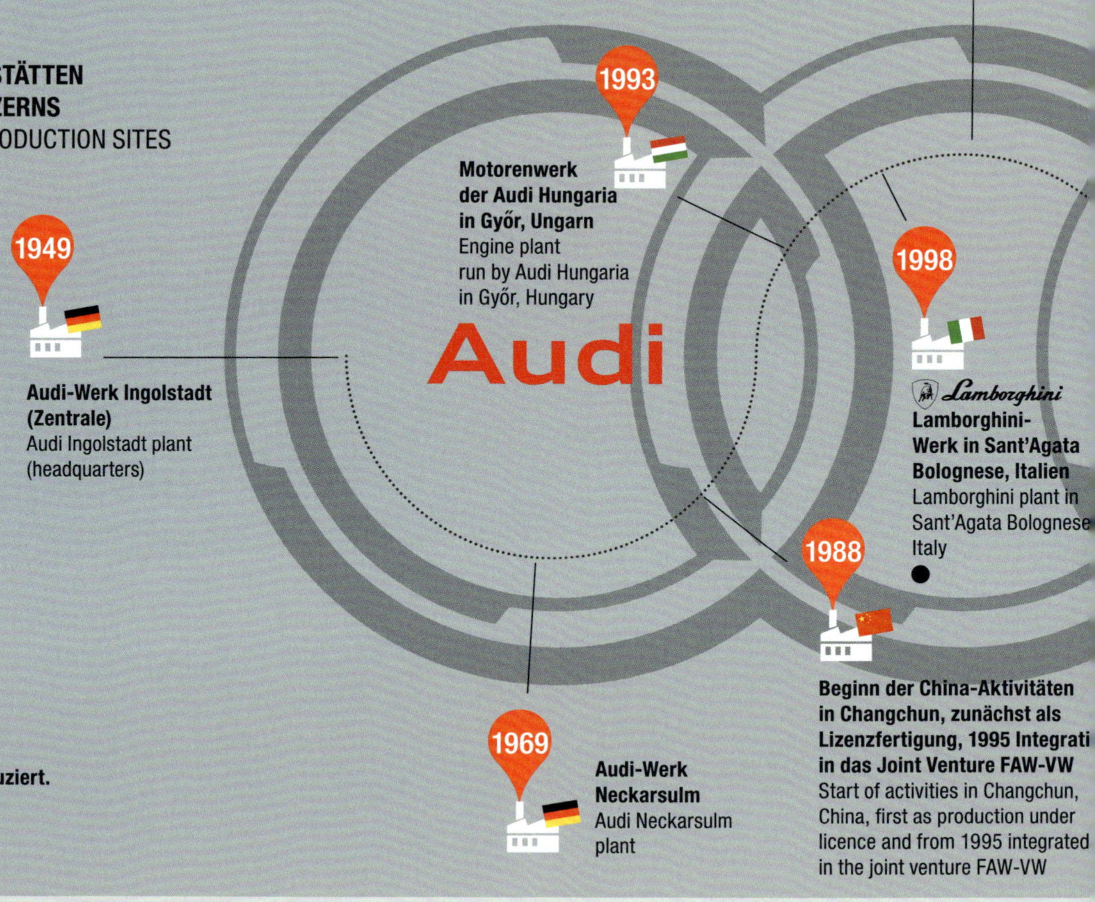

● **Hier werden keine Audi-Modelle produziert.**
No Audi models are produced here.

AUTOMOBILPRODUKTION IM IN- UND AUSLAND (INKL. LAMBORGHINI)
AUTOMOBILE PRODUCTION IN GERMANY AND ABROAD (INCL. LAMBORGHINI)

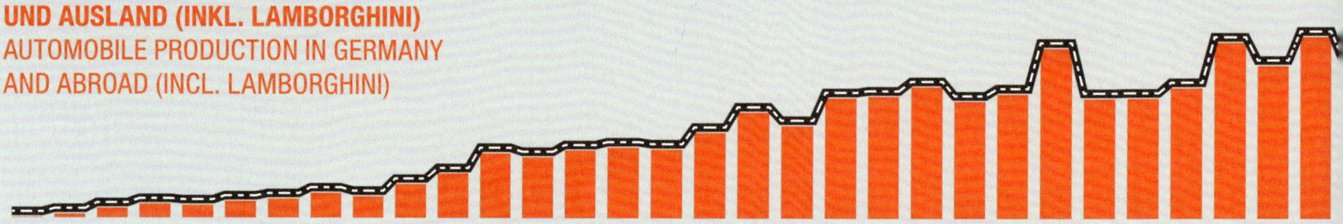

	gesamt / total
1949	504
1950	8.253
1951	22.393
1952	32.593
1953	29.762
1954	39.419
1955	45.061
1956	59.142
1957	51.074
1958	80.983
1959	107.388
1960	156.268
1961	146.867
1962	163.286
1963	170.287
1964	165.542
1965	205.910
1966	254.802
1967	222.672
1968	289.577
1969	293.673
1970	316.539
1971	282.200
1972	299.484
1973	409.793
1974	288.556
1975	289.561
1976	314.729
1977	424.171
1978	368.042
1979	438.505

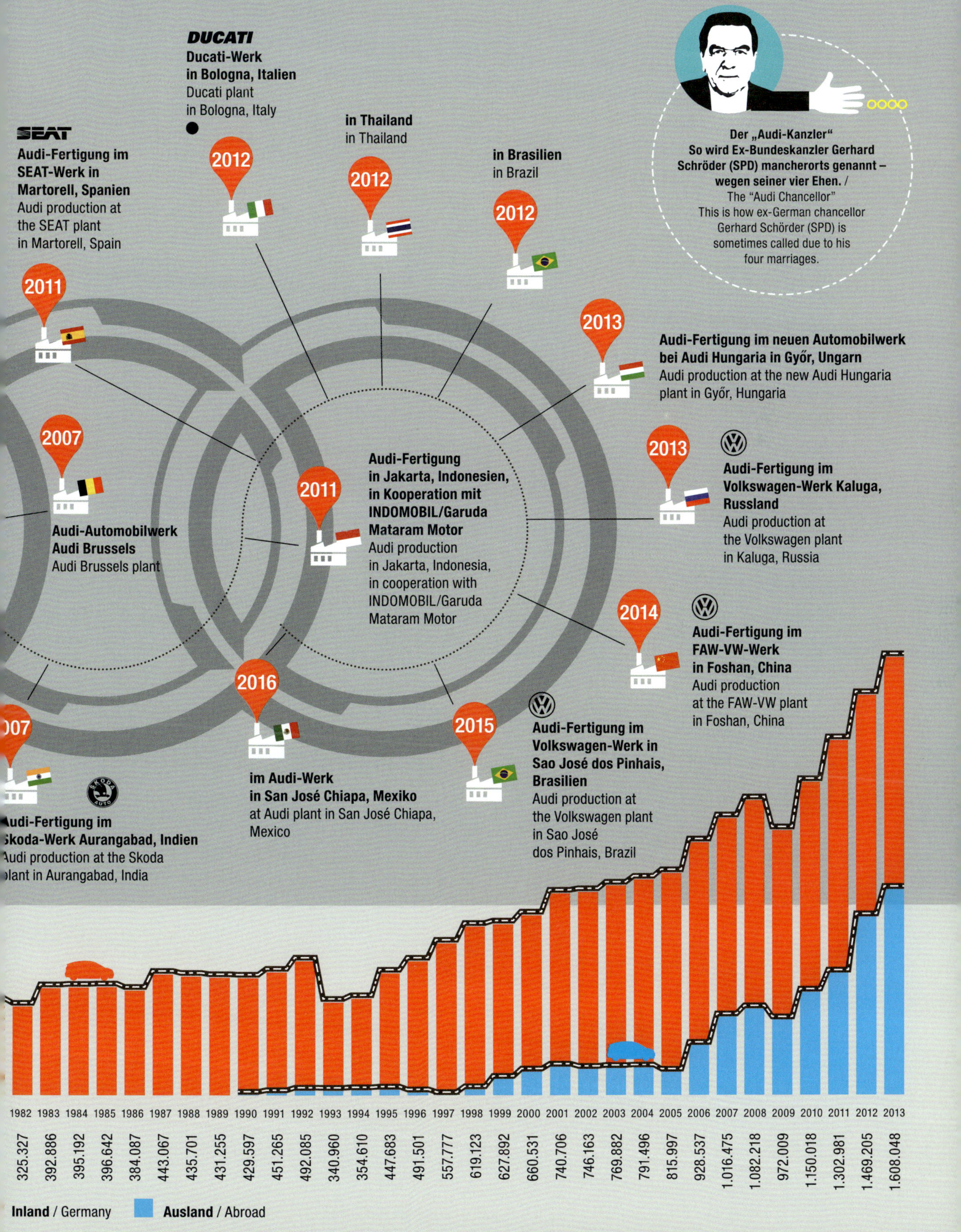
DUCATI
Ducati-Werk in Bologna, Italien
Ducati plant in Bologna, Italy
2012
in Thailand
in Thailand
2012
in Brasilien
in Brazil
2012
Der „Audi-Kanzler“
So wird Ex-Bundeskanzler Gerhard Schröder (SPD) mancherorts genannt – wegen seiner vier Ehen. /
The “Audi Chancellor”
This is how ex-German chancellor Gerhard Schörder (SPD) is sometimes called due to his four marriages.
SEAT
Audi-Fertigung im SEAT-Werk in Martorell, Spanien
Audi production at the SEAT plant in Martorell, Spain
2011
2013
Audi-Fertigung im neuen Automobilwerk bei Audi Hungaria in Győr, Ungarn
Audi production at the new Audi Hungaria plant in Győr, Hungaria
2007
Audi-Automobilwerk Audi Brussels
Audi Brussels plant
2011
Audi-Fertigung in Jakarta, Indonesien, in Kooperation mit INDOMOBIL/Garuda Mataram Motor
Audi production in Jakarta, Indonesia, in cooperation with INDOMOBIL/Garuda Mataram Motor
2013
Audi-Fertigung im Volkswagen-Werk Kaluga, Russland
Audi production at the Volkswagen plant in Kaluga, Russia
2014
Audi-Fertigung im FAW-VW-Werk in Foshan, China
Audi production at the FAW-VW plant in Foshan, China
2016
im Audi-Werk in San José Chiapa, Mexiko
at Audi plant in San José Chiapa, Mexico
2015
Audi-Fertigung im Volkswagen-Werk in Sao José dos Pinhais, Brasilien
Audi production at the Volkswagen plant in Sao José dos Pinhais, Brazil
007
udi-Fertigung im
koda-Werk Aurangabad, Indien
udi production at the Skoda
lant in Aurangabad, India
1982 325.327
1983 392.886
1984 395.192
1985 396.642
1986 384.087
1987 443.067
1988 435.701
1989 431.255
1990 429.597
1991 451.265
1992 492.085
1993 340.960
1994 354.610
1995 447.683
1996 491.501
1997 557.777
1998 619.123
1999 627.892
2000 660.531
2001 740.706
2002 746.163
2003 769.882
2004 791.496
2005 815.997
2006 928.537
2007 1.016.475
2008 1.082.218
2009 972.009
2010 1.150.018
2011 1.302.981
2012 1.469.205
2013 1.608.048
Inland / Germany
Ausland / Abroad

Heißer Kühler
Radiant radiators

Mitarbeiter Employees

Autoproduktion Automobile produc

BMW baut weltberühmte Autos mit einem einzigartigen Design – insbesondere wegen der „Doppel-Niere". Eine frontale Geschichte / BMW makes world-famous cars with exceptional design features – especially the unique "double kidney" grille. An up-front history

7.3.1916 Gründung der Bayerischen Motoren Werke AG, deren Anfänge auf die Rapp Motorenwerke und die Gustav Otto Flugmaschinenfabrik zurückgehen. Founding of the Bayerische Motoren Werke AG, which traces its origins to the Rapp Motorenwerke and the Gustav Otto aeroplane factory.

1916

RAPP MOTOR → BMW

1918 — **800** Mitarbeiter

Ausschließlich Produktion von Flugmotoren. Production of aircraft engines only

1920er-Jahre / 1920s

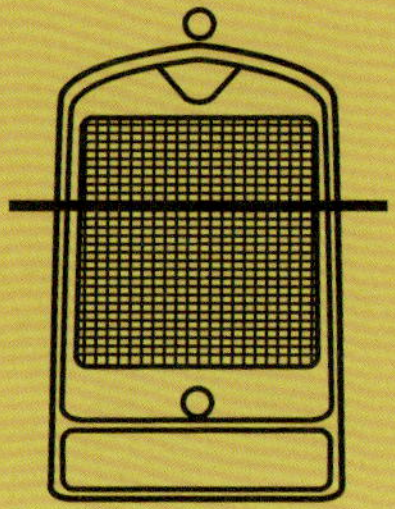

1929 BMW 3/15 — Mitarbeiter **3.309**, Autoproduktion **7.873**

1930er-Jahre / 1930s

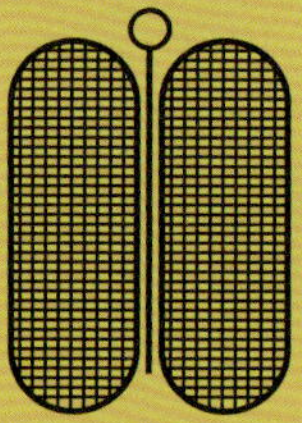

1933 BMW 303 — Mitarbeiter **6.514**, Autoproduktion **5.839**

1940er-Jahre / 1940s

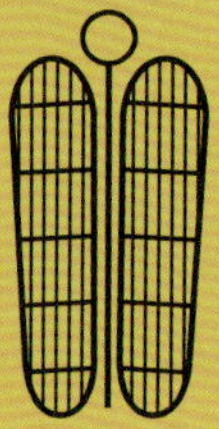

Bis / Until **1941 BMW 326** — Mitarbeiter **40.175**

Zwangsarbeit bei BMW: Herstellung von Flugmotoren für die Luftwaffe, Autoproduktion bis 1952 eingestellt / Forced labour at BMW: production aircraft engines for the Luftwaffe, automobile production suspended until 1952

1950er-Jahre / 1950s

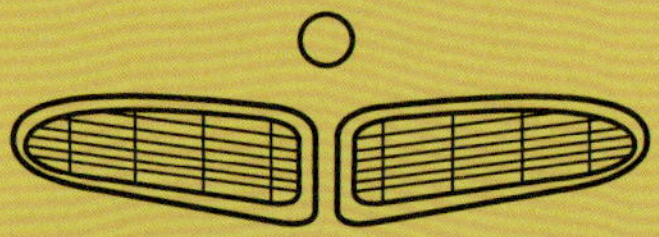

1956 Roadster BMW 507 — Mitarbeiter **5.757**, Autoproduktion **35.483**

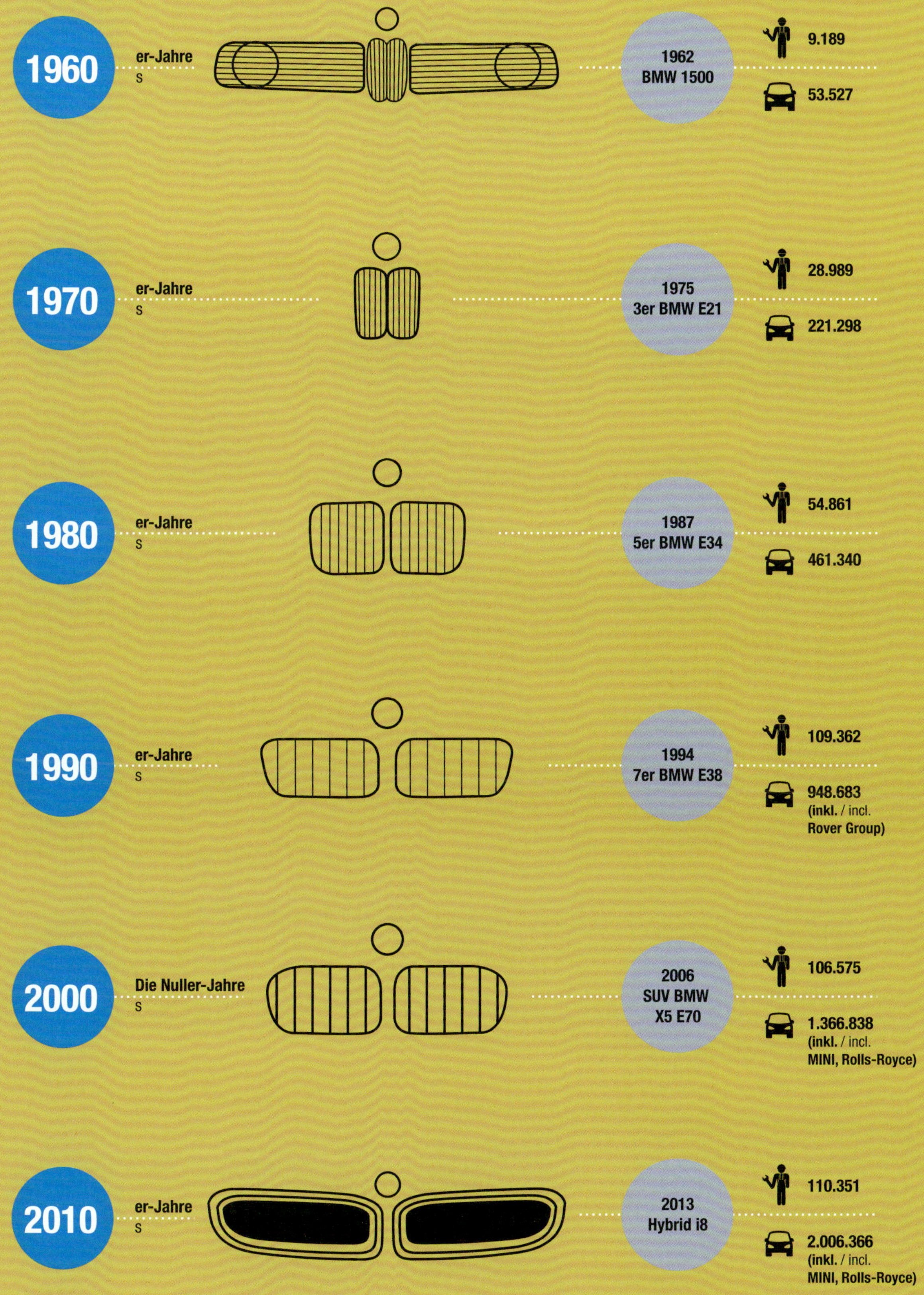
1960
er-Jahre
s
1962
BMW 1500
9.189
53.527
1970
er-Jahre
s
1975
3er BMW E21
28.989
221.298
1980
er-Jahre
s
1987
5er BMW E34
54.861
461.340
1990
er-Jahre
s
1994
7er BMW E38
109.362
948.683
(inkl. / incl.
Rover Group)
2000
Die Nuller-Jahre
s
2006
SUV BMW
X5 E70
106.575
1.366.838
(inkl. / incl.
MINI, Rolls-Royce)
2010
er-Jahre
s
2013
Hybrid i8
110.351
2.006.366
(inkl. / incl.
MINI, Rolls-Royce)

Ein Geben und Nehmen
Give and take

Das alte Rein-Raus-Spiel: Die wichtigsten Importe und Exporte des Freistaats /
In again, out again: Bavaria's prime imports and exports

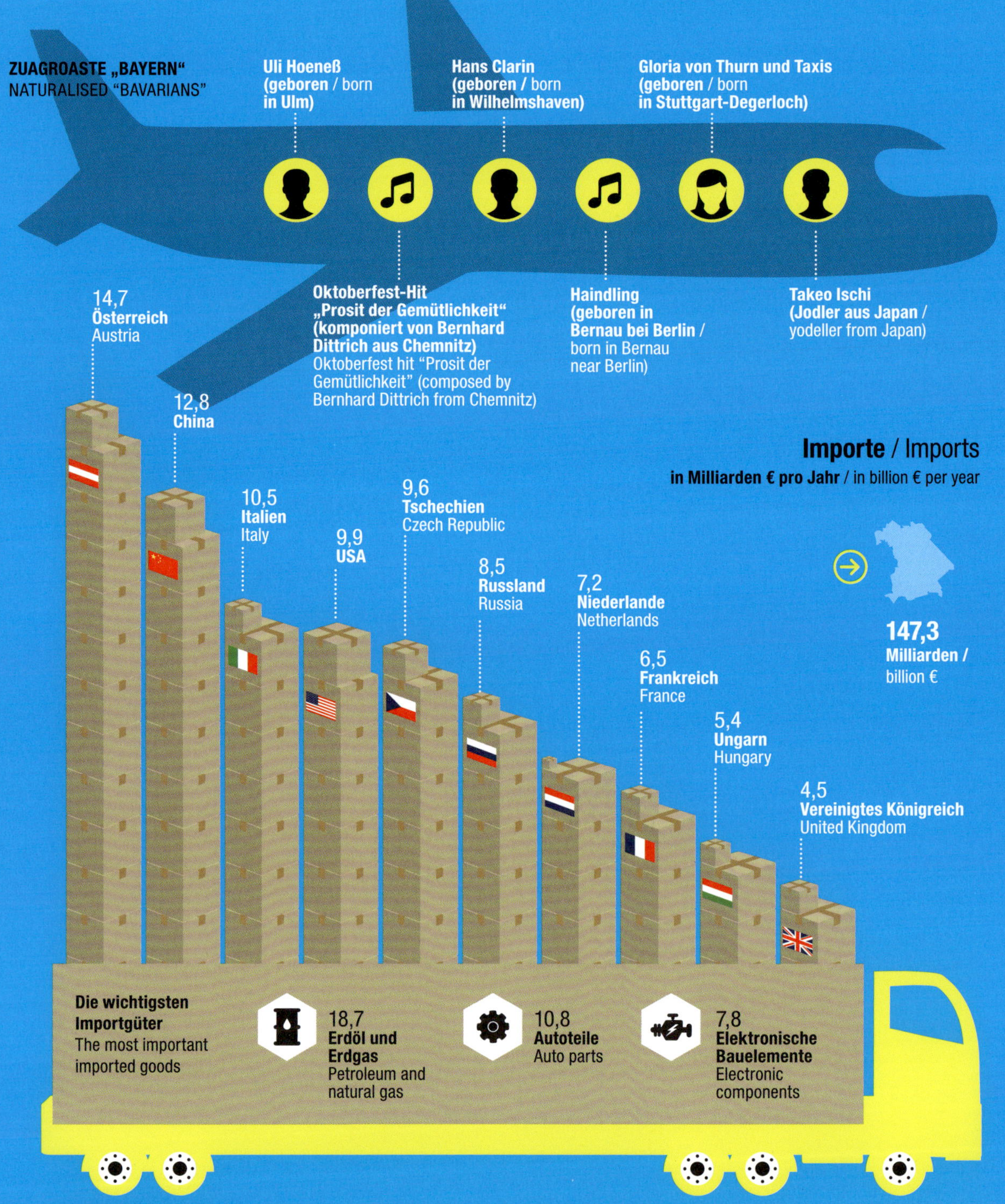

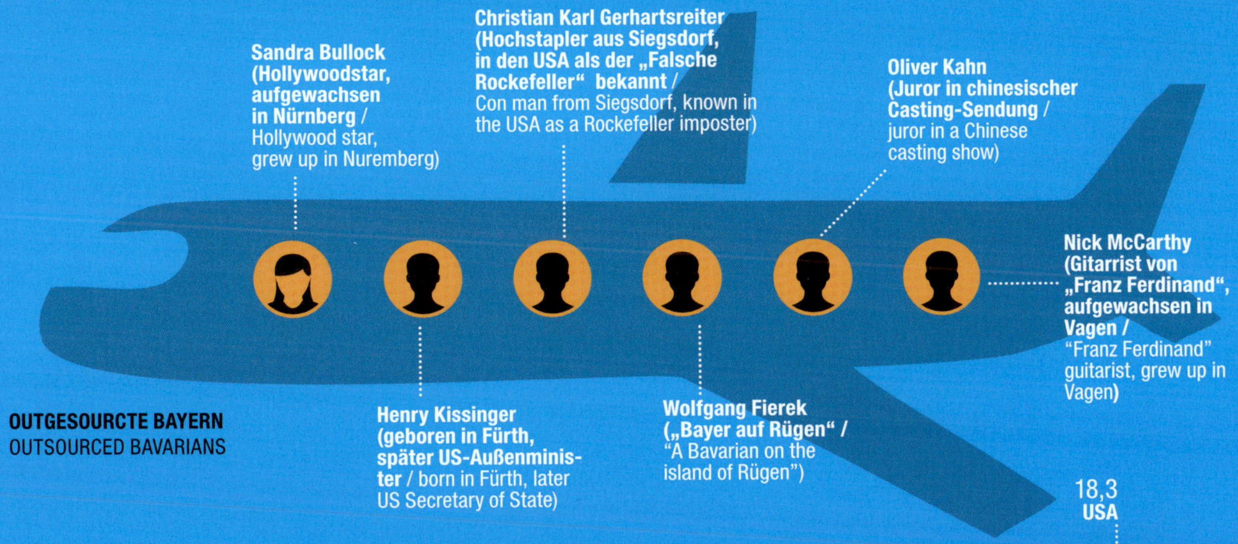
OUTGESOURCTE BAYERN
OUTSOURCED BAVARIANS
Sandra Bullock (Hollywoodstar, aufgewachsen in Nürnberg / Hollywood star, grew up in Nuremberg)
Christian Karl Gerhartsreiter (Hochstapler aus Siegsdorf, in den USA als der „Falsche Rockefeller“ bekannt / Con man from Siegsdorf, known in the USA as a Rockefeller imposter)
Oliver Kahn (Juror in chinesischer Casting-Sendung / juror in a Chinese casting show)
Nick McCarthy (Gitarrist von „Franz Ferdinand“, aufgewachsen in Vagen / “Franz Ferdinand” guitarist, grew up in Vagen)
Henry Kissinger (geboren in Fürth, später US-Außenminister / born in Fürth, later US Secretary of State)
Wolfgang Fierek („Bayer auf Rügen“ / “A Bavarian on the island of Rügen”)

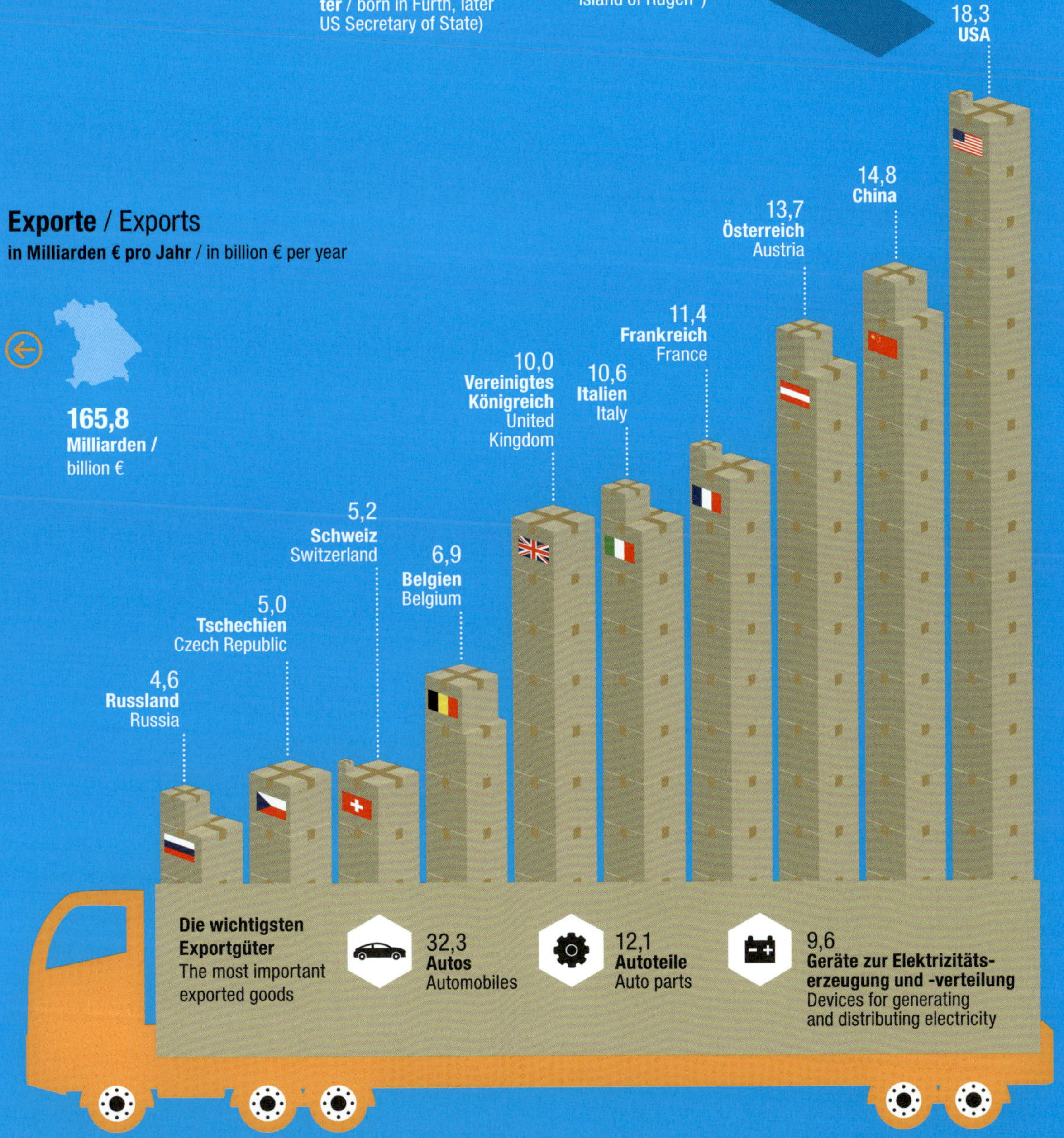
Exporte / Exports
in Milliarden € pro Jahr / in billion € per year
165,8 Milliarden / billion €
4,6 Russland Russia
5,0 Tschechien Czech Republic
5,2 Schweiz Switzerland
6,9 Belgien Belgium
10,0 Vereinigtes Königreich United Kingdom
10,6 Italien Italy
11,4 Frankreich France
13,7 Österreich Austria
14,8 China
18,3 USA
Die wichtigsten Exportgüter
The most important exported goods
32,3 Autos Automobiles
12,1 Autoteile Auto parts
9,6 Geräte zur Elektrizitätserzeugung und -verteilung
Devices for generating and distributing electricity

Über den Wolken
Up above the clouds

Der Verkehr am weiß-blauen Himmel /
Air traffic in the white-and-blue sky

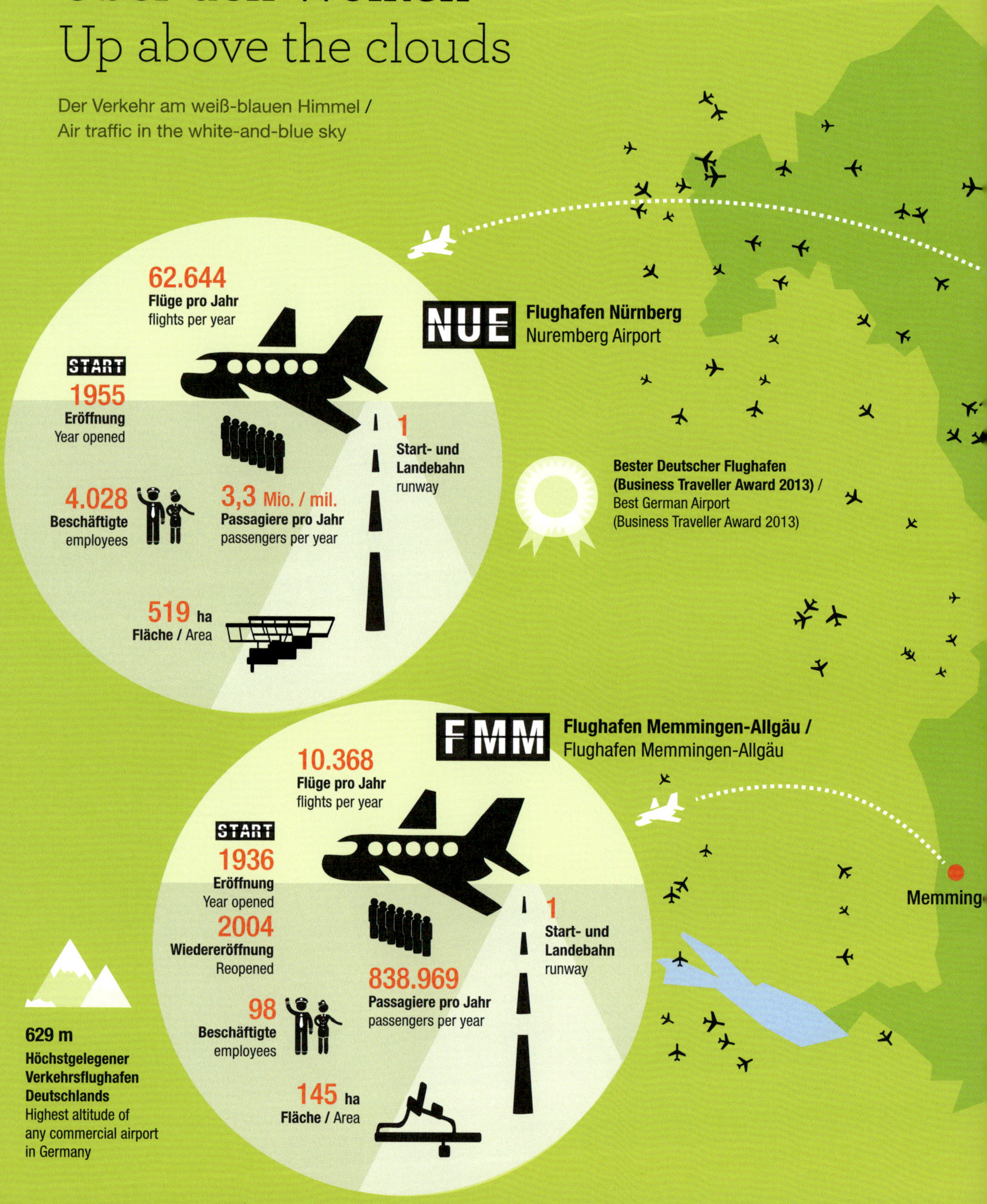

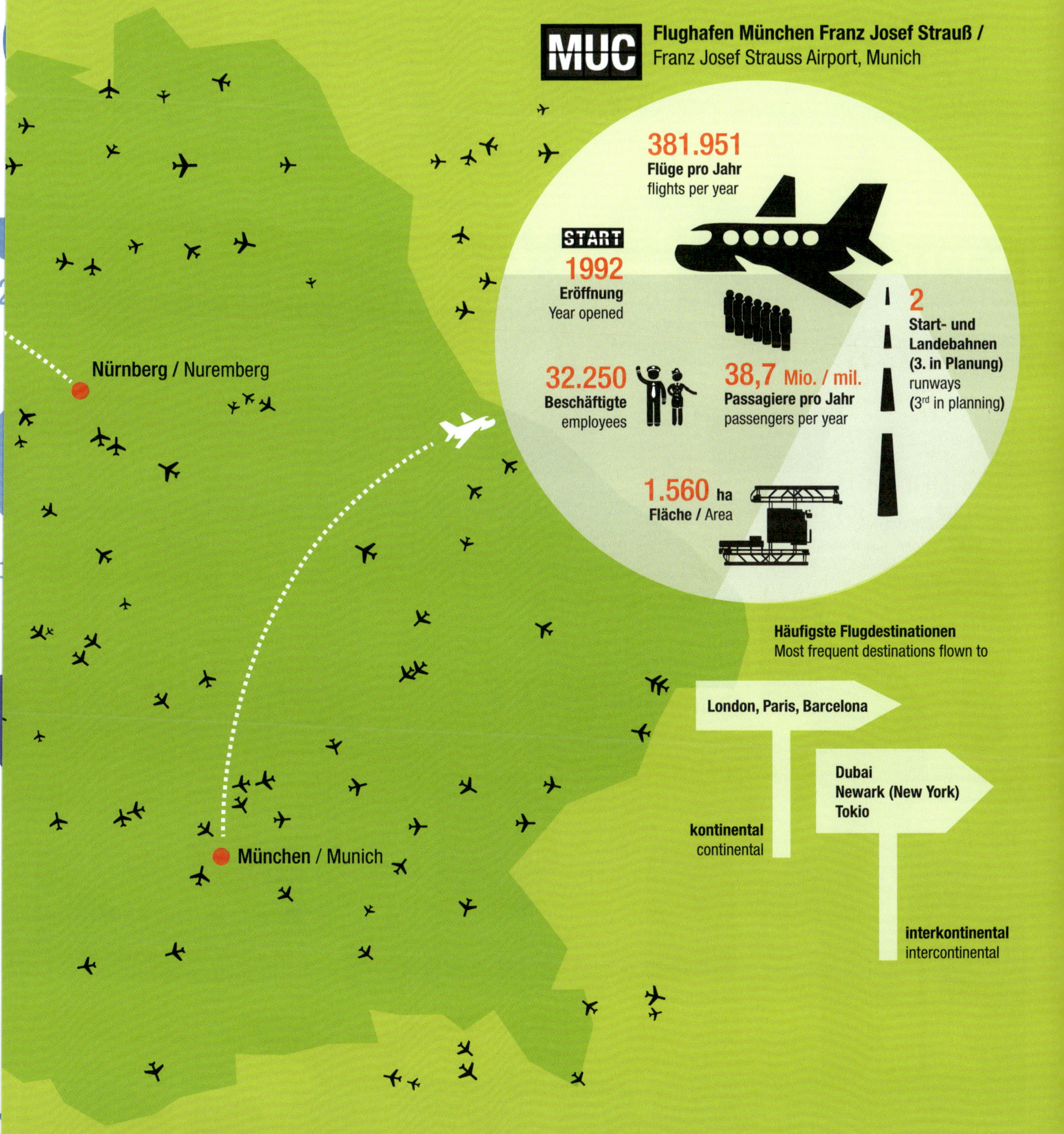

11:41 **Momentaufnahme des Luftraums über dem Freistaat an einem beliebigen Dienstag um 11:41 Uhr.**
Snapshot of the airspace over Bavaria at 11:41 am on a typical Tuesday

Flotter Dreier
Threesomes

Was verbirgt sich hinter den drei Begriffen? Der Bayern-Test für ehrgeizige Zuagroaste und heimische Gscheidhaferl / What might each set of three terms have in common? The Bavaria test for ambitious newcomers and native know-it-alls

1 + 2 + 3 = 1 (6 letters)

Audi + ERC + Frankenstein = 2 (10 letters)

Flo + Peter + Rüde = 3

Batic + Leitmayr + 5er BMW = 4

Weißwein White wine + **Zitronenlimo** Lemonade + **Kirschlikör** Cherry liqueur = 5 (11 letters)

Kaiserdom Imperial Cathedral + **Altstadt** Historic centre + **Brose Baskets** = 6 (7 letters)

Franz-Josef + Richard + Levi =

7

Stefan Mross + Florian Silbereisen + Margot & Maria Hellwig =

8

Rosi + Christian + Felix =

9

Hans + Sophie + Mehmet =

10

Wasser + Malz + Hopfen =

Water + Malt + Hops

11

INA + FAG + LUK =

12

Mittelalter + Amerikaner + Japaner =

Middle Ages + Americans + Japanese

13

Hans + Stofferl + Michael =

14

Lösungen / Solutions: **1** Gsuffa! (Bottoms up!), **2** Ingolstadt, **3** Sportfreunde Stiller, **4** Tatort aus München (Tatort TV crime show from Munich), **5** Laternenmaß (Laternemass cocktail), **6** Bamberg, **7** Strauss, **8** Musikantenstadl (Stars of Musikantenstadl folk music TV show), **9** Neureuther, **10** Scholl, **11** Reinheitsgebot (Germany purity law for beer) **12** Schaeffler, **13** Rothenburg ob der Tauber, **14** Biermösl Blosn

Wahre Größe

Size matters

Bayerisches in Originalgröße / Bavarian items in their original size

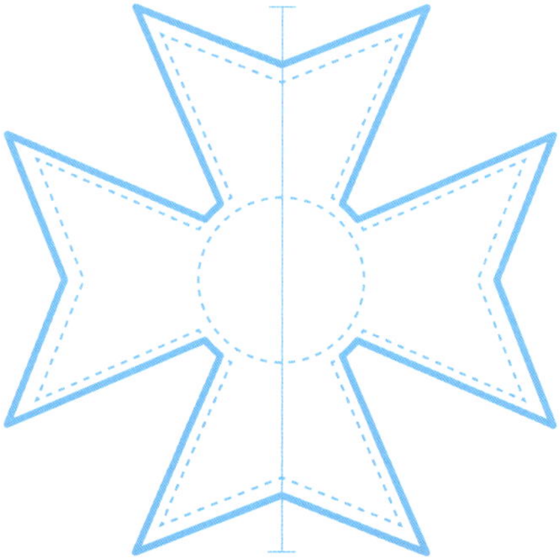

Bayerischer Verdienstorden
Bavarian Order of Merit
5,5 cm

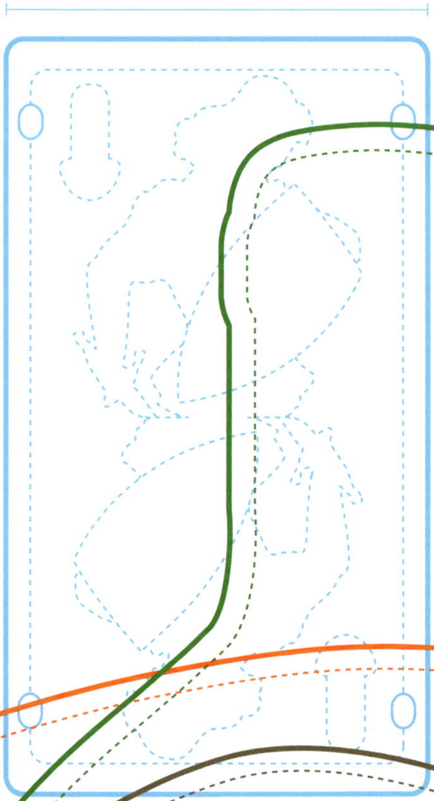

Eichel-Ober
(Schafkopf-Trumpf)
Eichel Ober
(trump card in Schafkopf)
5,6 cm x 10 cm

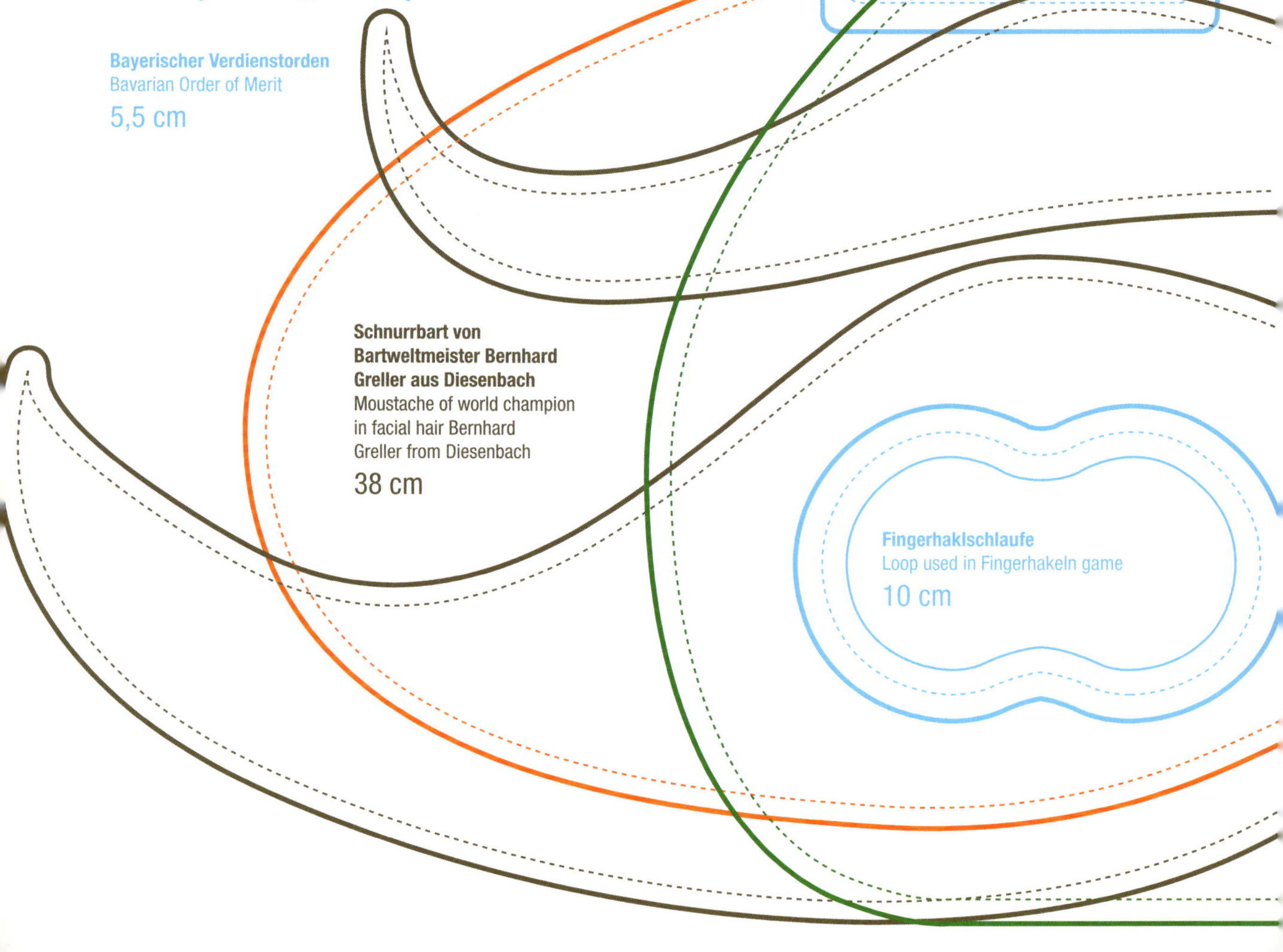

Schnurrbart von Bartweltmeister Bernhard Greller aus Diesenbach
Moustache of world champion in facial hair Bernhard Greller from Diesenbach
38 cm

Fingerhaklschlaufe
Loop used in Fingerhakeln game
10 cm

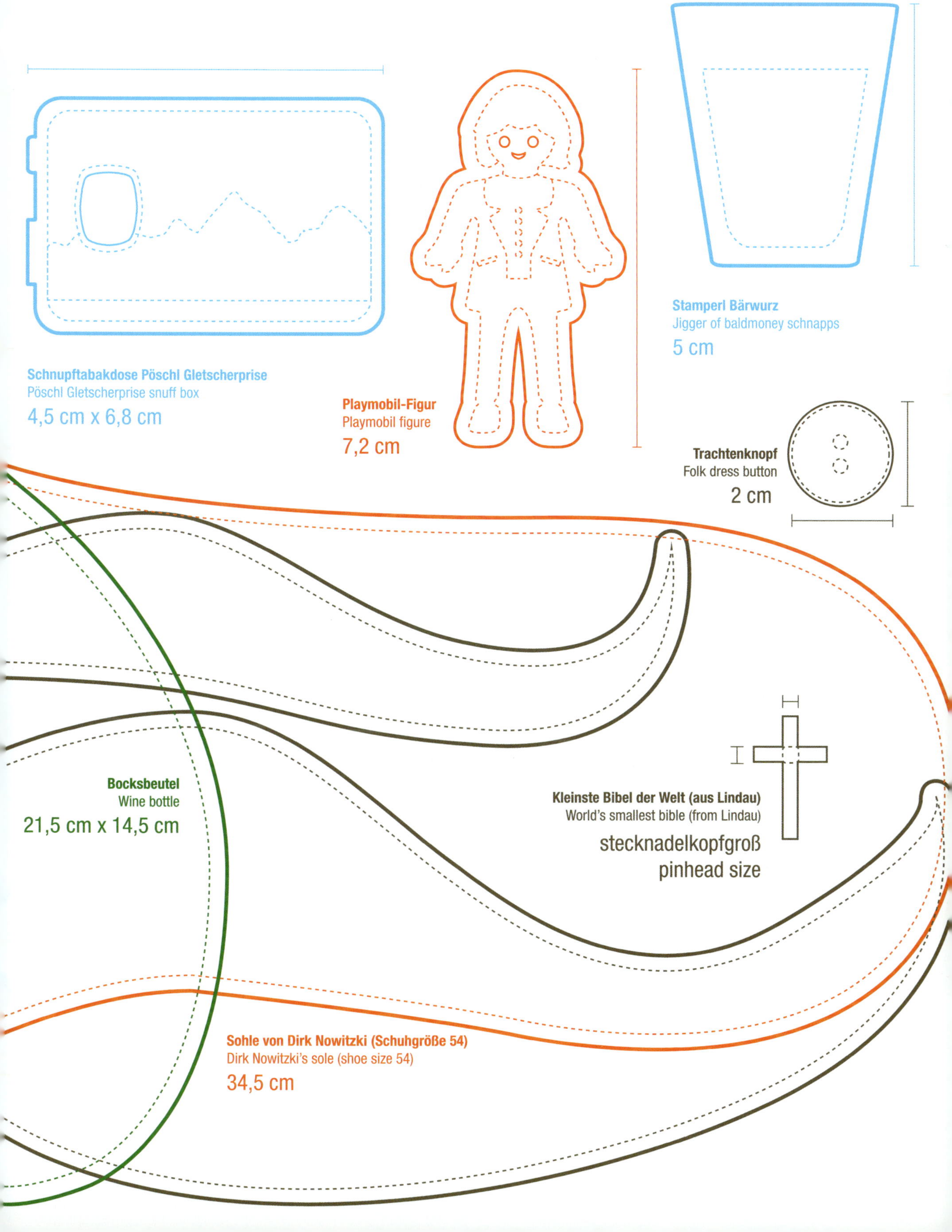

Schnupftabakdose Pöschl Gletscherprise
Pöschl Gletscherprise snuff box
4,5 cm x 6,8 cm
Playmobil-Figur
Playmobil figure
7,2 cm
Stamperl Bärwurz
Jigger of baldmoney schnapps
5 cm
Trachtenknopf
Folk dress button
2 cm
Kleinste Bibel der Welt (aus Lindau)
World's smallest bible (from Lindau)
stecknadelkopfgroß
pinhead size
Bocksbeutel
Wine bottle
21,5 cm x 14,5 cm
Sohle von Dirk Nowitzki (Schuhgröße 54)
Dirk Nowitzki's sole (shoe size 54)
34,5 cm

Lang lang
It’s a long, long road

Und jetzt alle: Strecken! / And now everyone: stretch!

Kaufingerstr.

220 m
Kaufingerstraße (München / Munich**)**

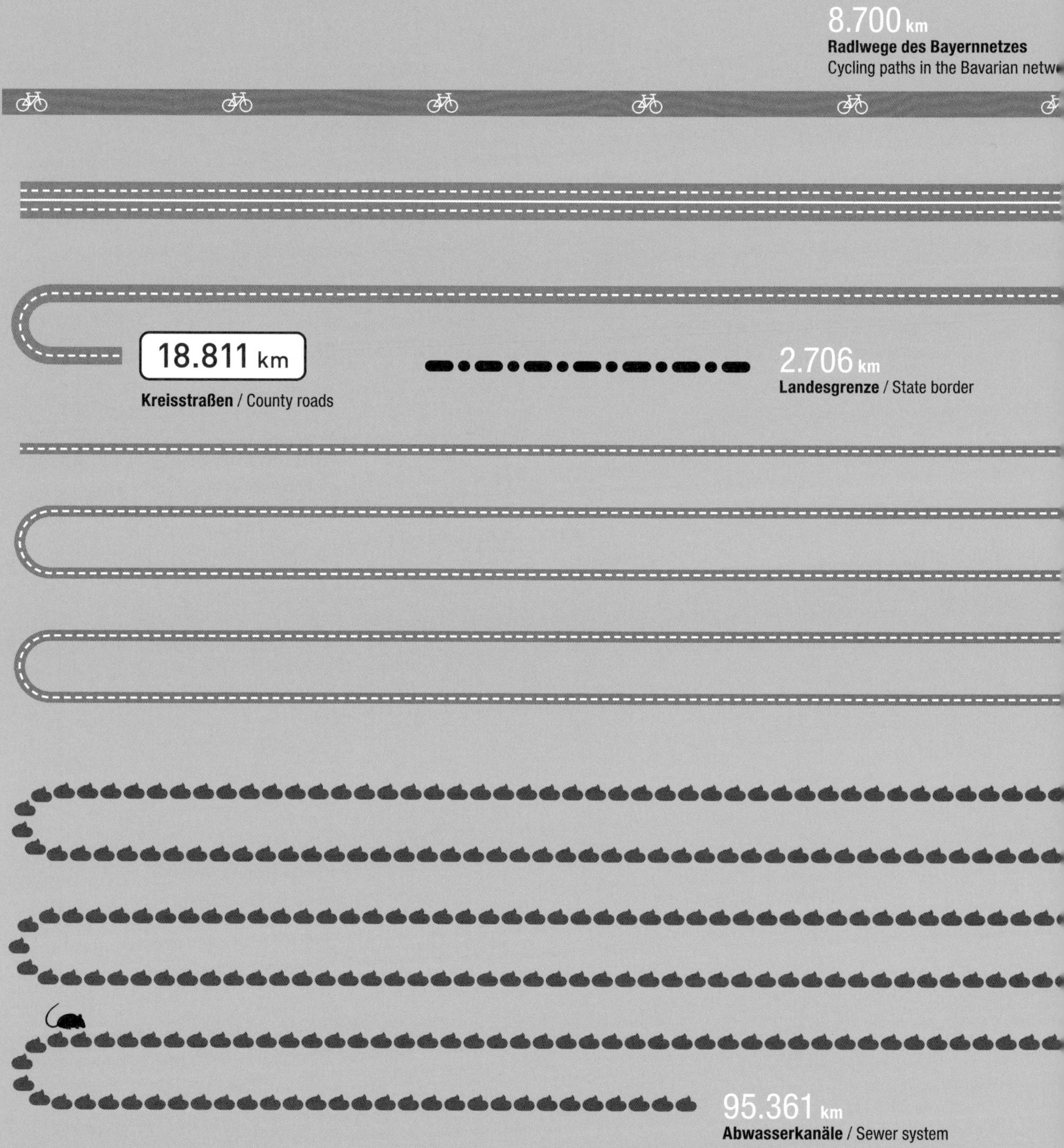

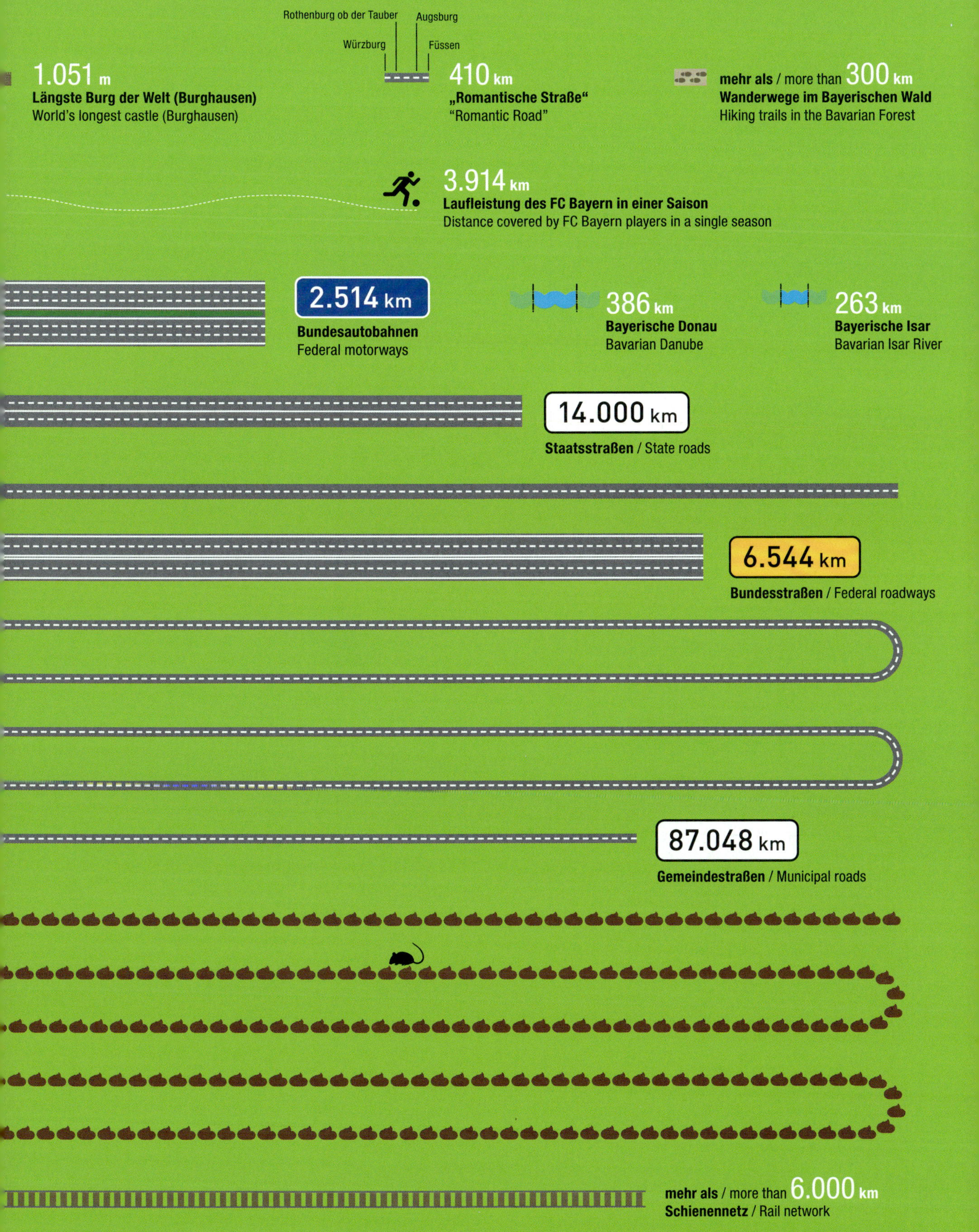

Rothenburg ob der Tauber
Augsburg
Würzburg
Füssen
1.051 m
Längste Burg der Welt (Burghausen)
World's longest castle (Burghausen)
410 km
„Romantische Straße“
“Romantic Road”
mehr als / more than 300 km
Wanderwege im Bayerischen Wald
Hiking trails in the Bavarian Forest
3.914 km
Laufleistung des FC Bayern in einer Saison
Distance covered by FC Bayern players in a single season
2.514 km
Bundesautobahnen
Federal motorways
386 km
Bayerische Donau
Bavarian Danube
263 km
Bayerische Isar
Bavarian Isar River
14.000 km
Staatsstraßen / State roads
6.544 km
Bundesstraßen / Federal roadways
87.048 km
Gemeindestraßen / Municipal roads
mehr als / more than 6.000 km
Schienennetz / Rail network

Wer suchet ...
Seek ...

Die jüngere Geschichte Bayerns im Trend: Wann wurden die folgenden Begriffe besonders häufig gegoogelt? Und warum? / Bavaria's recent history trending on the Web: When were the following terms googled most often? And why?

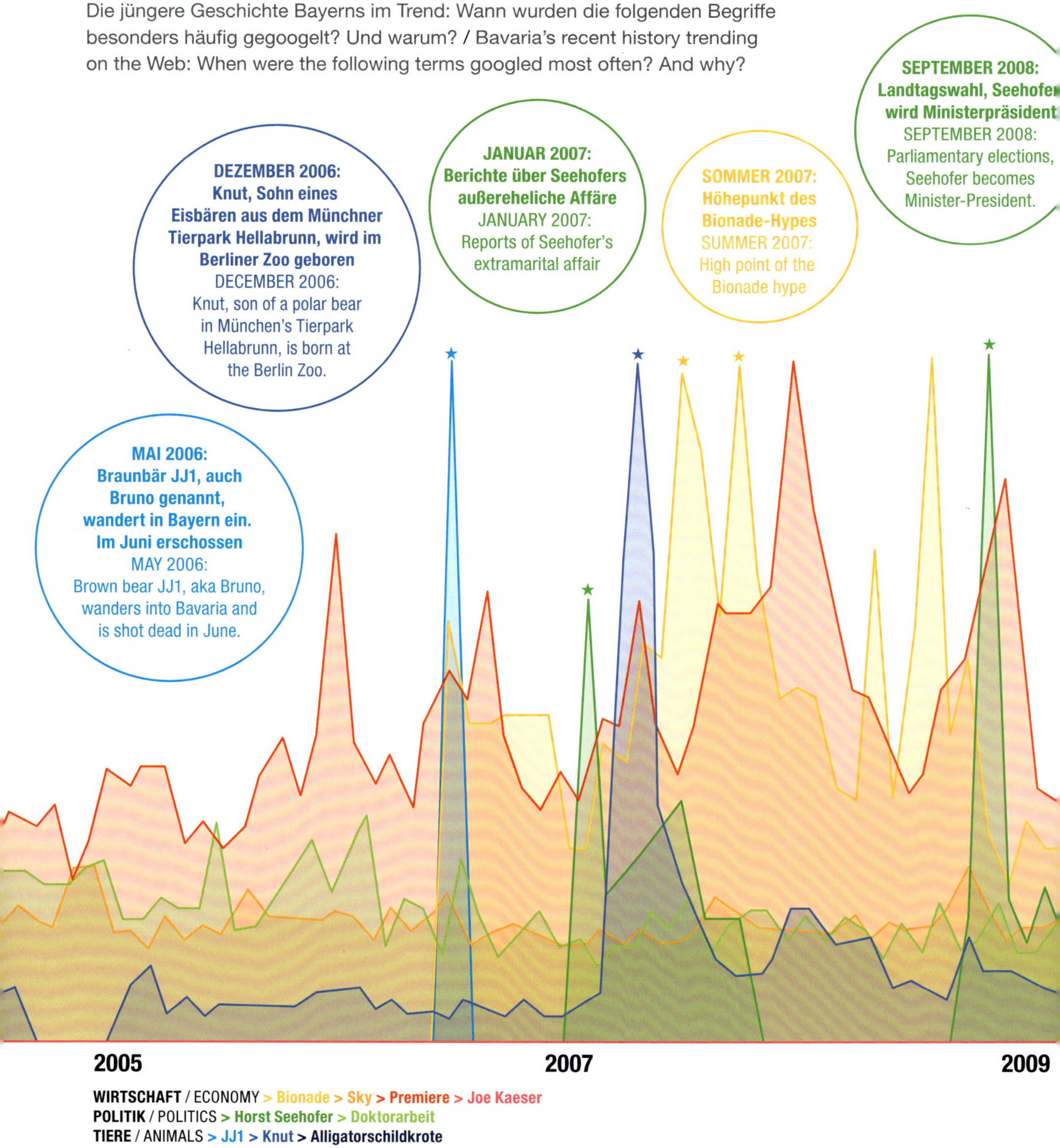

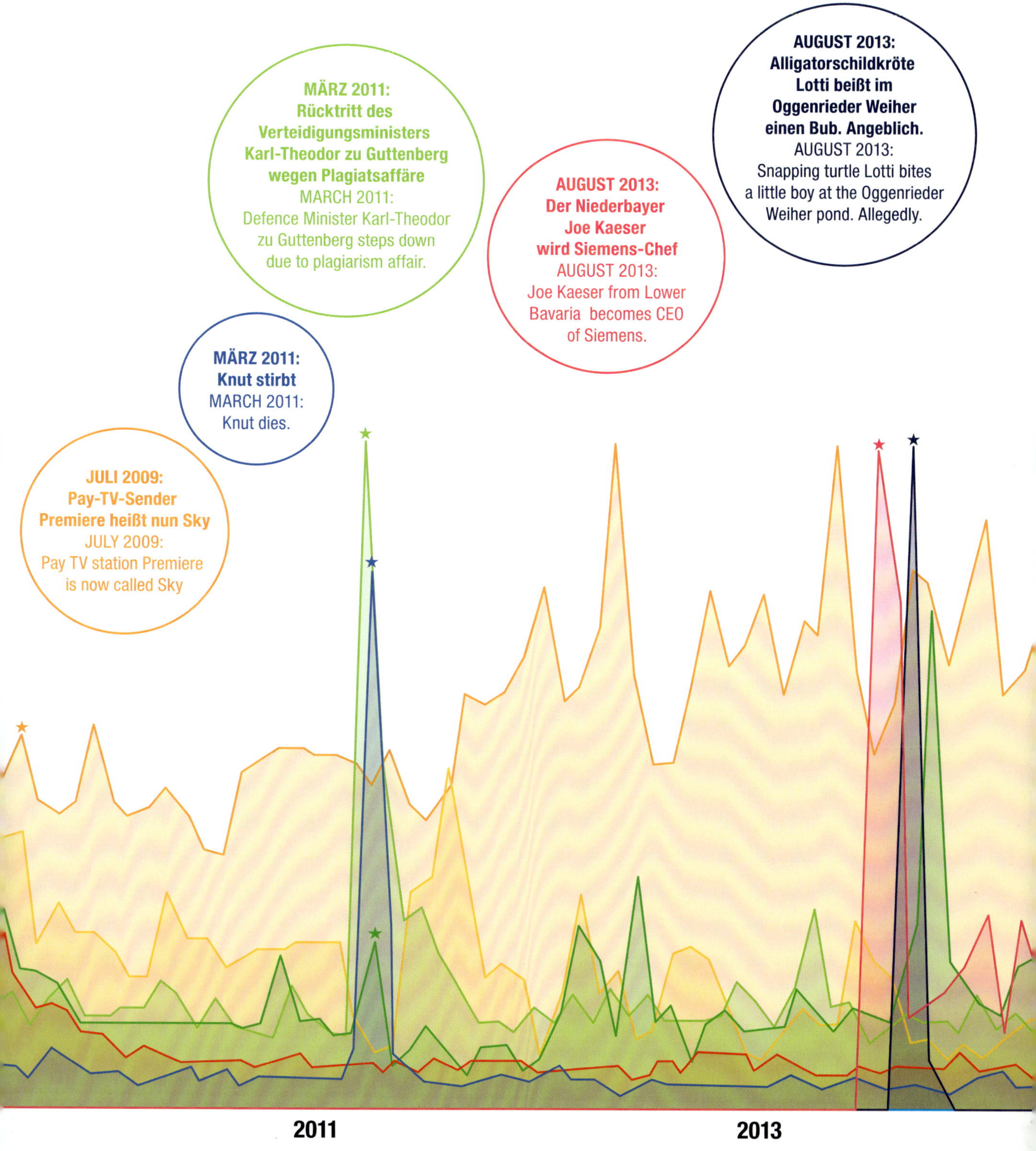

MÄRZ 2011:
Rücktritt des Verteidigungsministers Karl-Theodor zu Guttenberg wegen Plagiatsaffäre
MARCH 2011:
Defence Minister Karl-Theodor zu Guttenberg steps down due to plagiarism affair.
AUGUST 2013:
Alligatorschildkröte Lotti beißt im Oggenrieder Weiher einen Bub. Angeblich.
AUGUST 2013:
Snapping turtle Lotti bites a little boy at the Oggenrieder Weiher pond. Allegedly.
AUGUST 2013:
Der Niederbayer Joe Kaeser wird Siemens-Chef
AUGUST 2013:
Joe Kaeser from Lower Bavaria becomes CEO of Siemens.
MÄRZ 2011:
Knut stirbt
MARCH 2011:
Knut dies.
JULI 2009:
Pay-TV-Sender Premiere heißt nun Sky
JULY 2009:
Pay TV station Premiere is now called Sky
2011
2013

... der findet.
... and you shall find.

* **Anmerkung: Die Kurven zeigen nicht die absolute Häufigkeit der Suchanfragen an, sondern nur deren Trend in Bayern.**
Note: The curves do not show the absolute frequency of searches but rather only the trends in Bavaria.

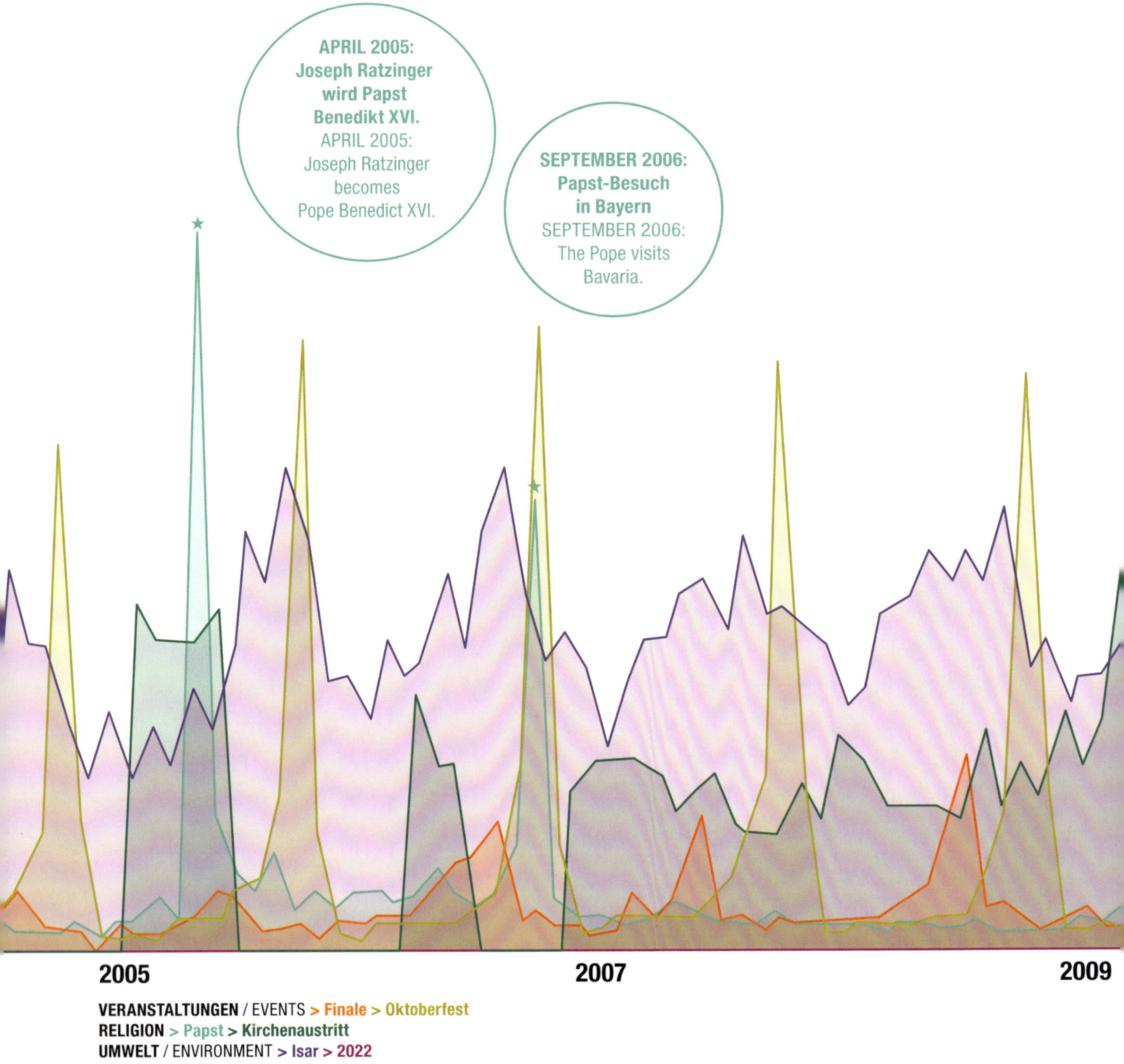

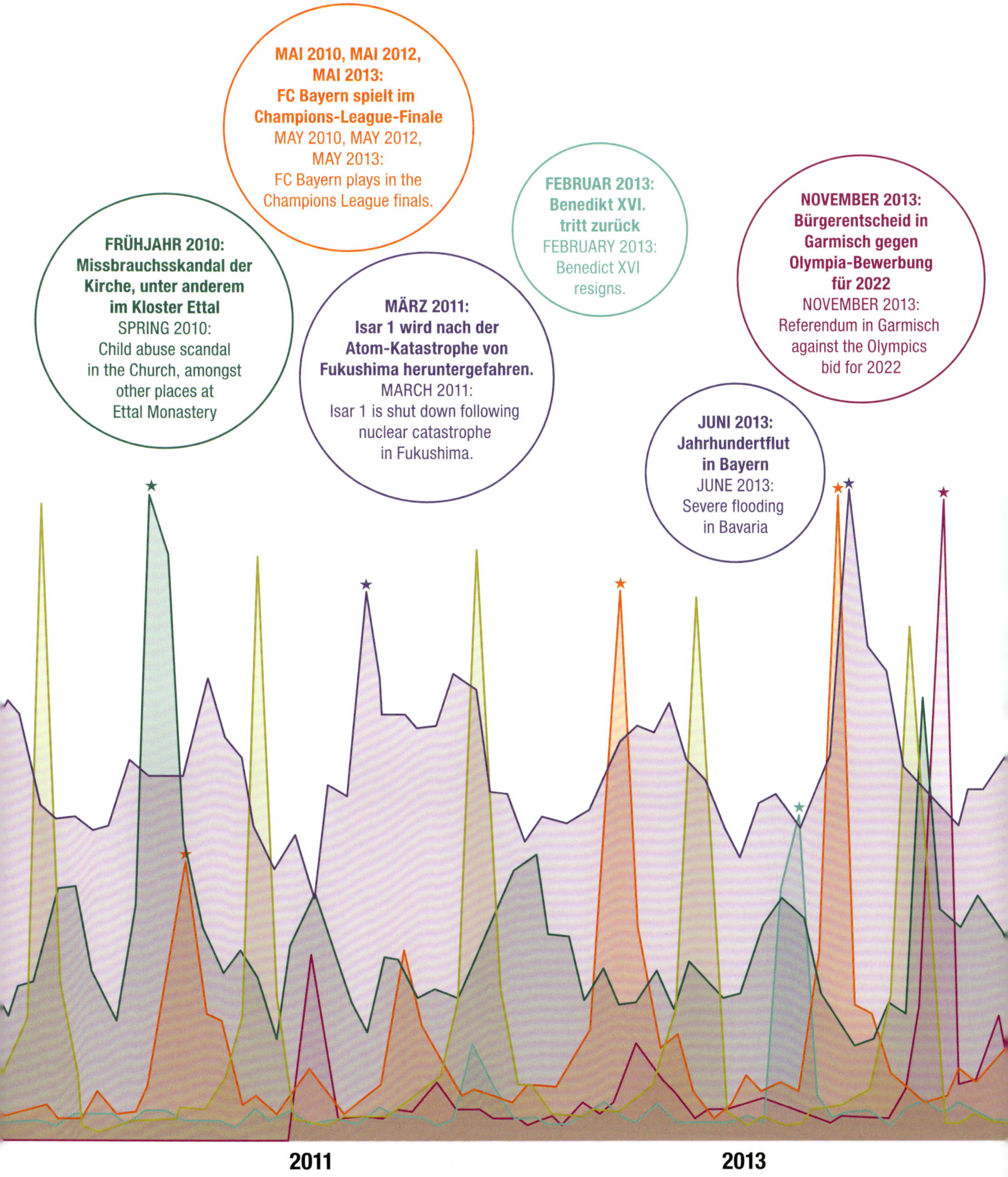

MAI 2010, MAI 2012, MAI 2013: FC Bayern spielt im Champions-League-Finale
MAY 2010, MAY 2012, MAY 2013: FC Bayern plays in the Champions League finals.
FEBRUAR 2013: Benedikt XVI. tritt zurück
FEBRUARY 2013: Benedict XVI resigns.
NOVEMBER 2013: Bürgerentscheid in Garmisch gegen Olympia-Bewerbung für 2022
NOVEMBER 2013: Referendum in Garmisch against the Olympics bid for 2022
FRÜHJAHR 2010: Missbrauchsskandal der Kirche, unter anderem im Kloster Ettal
SPRING 2010: Child abuse scandal in the Church, amongst other places at Ettal Monastery
MÄRZ 2011: Isar 1 wird nach der Atom-Katastrophe von Fukushima heruntergefahren.
MARCH 2011: Isar 1 is shut down following nuclear catastrophe in Fukushima.
JUNI 2013: Jahrhundertflut in Bayern
JUNE 2013: Severe flooding in Bavaria
2011
2013

Der bayerische Kalender
The Bavarian calendar

JANUAR / JANUARY

1	Hans-Joachim „Strietzel“ Stuck (* 1951)	
2	Willi Graf (1918–1943)	*
3	Otto Beisheim (1924–2013)	*
4	Luise Kinseher (* 1969)	
5	Uli Hoeneß (* 1952 in Ulm)	*
6	Walter Sedlmayr (1929–1990)	
7	Friedrich Ani (* 1959)	
8	Gret Palucca (1902–1993)	
9	Waltraud Meier (* 1956)	
10	Maximilian Brückner (* 1979)	
11	Anna „Anni“ Friesinger-Postma (* 1977)	
12	Ottmar Hitzfeld (* 1949)	*
13	Daniel Kehlmann (* 1975)	
14	Patricia Schäfer (* 1968)	
15	Franz Xaver Bogner (* 1949)	
16	Michl Lang (1899–1979)	
17	Ludwig Wilhelm in Bayern (1884–1968)	
18	Christa Berndl (* 1932)	
19	Thomas Gsella (* 1958)	*
20	Axel Hacke (* 1956)	*
21	Ludwig Thoma (1867–1921)	
22	Jenny Jürgens (* 1967)	
23	Willy Bogner (* 1942)	
24	Joseph Vilsmaier (* 1939)	
25	Roy Black (* 1943)	
26	Heinrich von Pierer (* 1941)	
27	Günter Gloser (* 1950)	
28	Hans-Jürgen Bäumler (* 1942)	
29	Urban Mangold (* 1963)	
30	Lorenz-Günther Köstner (* 1952)	
31	Rudolf Mößbauer (1929–2011)	

FEBRUAR / FEBRUARY

1	Raphael Schäfer (* 1979)	*
2	Adolf Gustav Rupprecht Maximilian „Gustl“ Bayrhammer (1922–1993)	
3	Anette Kolb (* 1870)	
4	Ludwig Erhard (1897–1977)	
5	Franz Carl Spitzweg (1808–1885)	
6	Eva Braun (1912–1945)	
7	Wilhelm „Willy“ Bogner Senior (1909–1977)	
8	Franz Marc (1880–1916)	
9	Magdalena Neuner (* 1987)	
10	Bertolt Brecht (1898–1956)	
11	Cleo Kretschmer (* 1951)	
12	Gustl Bayrhammer (1922–1993)	
13	Andrea Kaiser (* 1982)	
14	Martin Bader (* 1968)	*
15	Johann Elias Ridinger (1698–1767)	*
16	Erwin Pelzig (* 1960)	
17	Lola Montez (1821–1861)	*
18	Heini Müller (* 1934)	
19	Cosmic Baby (* 1963)	*
20	Heidemarie Wright (* 1951)	*
21	Max von Thun (* 1977)	
22	Theodor „Theo“ Waigel (* 1939)	
23	Mariae Gloria von Thurn und Taxis (* 1960)	*
24	Georg Späth (* 1981)	*
25	Franz Xaver Kroetz (* 1946)	
26	Martina Schwarzmann (* 1979)	
27	Rudolf Kraus (* 1941)	
28	Josef Dieter „Sepp“ Maier (* 1944)	
29	Vanessa Jung (* 1980)	

* **Zuagroaste „Bayern“** / Naturalised “Bavarians”

MÄRZ / MARCH

1	Monika Pflug (* 1954)	
2	Helga Ursula „Uschi“ Glas (* 1944)	
3	Takeo Ischi (* 1947)	
4	Friedrich Wilhelm Walther von Walderstötten (1805–1889)	
5	Barbara Schöneberger (* 1974)	
6	Jakob Fugger (1459–1525)	
7	Joseph von Fraunhofer (1787–1826)	
8	Franziska Fischer (1897–1972)	
9	Roy Makaay (* 1975)	*
10	Hans Drachsler (1916–1996)	
11	Beppo Brem (1906–1990)	
12	Hans Drachsler (1916–1996)	
13	Andreas „Andy“ Köpke (* 1962)	*
14	Florian Hahn (* 1974)	
15	Anna von Bayern (* 1978)	
16	Georg Simon Ohm (1789–1854)	
17	Claus Reitmaier (* 1964)	
18	Michaela May (* 1952)	
19	Hannes Aigner (* 1989)	
20	Susanne Berckheimer (* 1978)	
21	Jean Paul (* 1763)	
22	Helmut Fleischer (* 1964)	
23	Stefan Kellner (* 1962)	
24	Philipp Petzschner (* 1984)	
25	Karl-Heinz Schreiber (* 1934)	*
26	Patrick Süskind (* 1949)	
27	Toni Berger (1921–2005)	
28	Therese Angeloff (1911–1985)	
29	Alexander Moritz Frey (1881–1957)	
30	Hans Zach (* 1949)	
31	Heinz Putzhammer (1941–2006)	

Barbara Schöneberger

Senta Berger

Doris Dörrie

Karl Valentin

APRIL / APRIL

1	Hermann Otto II. von Limburg Styrum (1646–1704)	
2	Siegfried Rauch (* 1942)	
3	Michael Mittermeier (* 1966)	
4	Karl Obermayr (1931–1985)	
5	Roman Herzog (* 1934)	
6	Michael Walther der Ältere (1593–1662)	
7	Erich „Rick“ Goldmann (* 1976)	
8	Reinhold Albert Aman (* 1936)	
9	Christian Anton Meyer (1922–2005)	
10	Georg Nüßlein (* 1969)	
11	Bernd Eichinger (1949–2011)	
12	Tobias Angerer (* 1977)	
13	Lou Bega (* 1975)	
14	Luitpold Prinz von Bayern (* 1951)	
15	Adam von Herberstorff (1585–1629)	*
16	Benedikt XVI. (Joseph Aloisius Ratzinger) (* 1927)	
17	Rudolf Schüler (1906–1988)	*
18	Manfred Schwabl (* 1966)	
19	Django Asül (* 1972)	
20	Carl Gottlob Beck (1733–1802)	*
21	Georg Kronawitter (* 1928)	
22	Theo Waigel (* 1939)	
23	Hansl Krönauer (1932–2011)	
24	Sabina von Bayern (* 1492)	
25	Francis Fulton-Smith (* 1966)	
26	Josef Bierbichler (* 1948)	
27	Lars & Sven Bender (* 1989)	
28	Heinrich Müller (1900–1945)	
29	Michael „Bully“ Herbig (* 1968)	
30	Kaspar Hauser (1812–1833)	

MAI / MAY

1	Diego Contento (* 1990)	
2	Alfons Schuhbeck (* 1949)	
3	Albrecht von Bayern (* 1905)	
4	Julius Seyler (1873–1955)	
5	Dagmar Wöhrl (* 1954)	
6	Christian Morgenstern (1871–1914)	
7	Max Grundig (1908–1989)	
8	Eva-Maria May (* 1985)	
9	Johannes Singhammer (* 1953)	
10	Katja Seizinger (Katja Weber) (* 1972)	*
11	Max Morlock (1925–1994)	
12	Hans Leyendecker (* 1949)	
13	Senta Berger (* 1941)	*
14	Marquard Sebastian Schenk von Stauffenberg (1644–1693)	
15	Claudia Benedikta Roth (* 1955)	
16	Achim Bröger (* 1944)	
17	Sebastian Anton Kneipp (1821–1897)	
18	Thomas Gottschalk (* 1950)	
19	Felix Otto (* 1966)	
20	Gerd Rubenbauer (* 1948)	
21	Albrecht Dürer der Jüngere (1471–1528)	
22	Richard Wagner (1813–1883)	*
23	Henry (Heinz) Alfred Kissinger (* 1923)	
24	Rainald Goetz (* 1954)	
25	Hans Jakob „Jack“ Kissinger (* 1921)	
26	Doris Dörrie (* 1955)	*
27	Maximilian I. Joseph (1756–1825)	*
28	Claudia Koreck (* 1986)	
29	Elyas M'Barek (* 1982)	
30	Rita Falk (* 1964)	
31	Rainer Werner Fassbinder (1945–1982)	

JUNI / JUNE

1	Konstantin Wecker (* 1947)	
2	Caroline Link (* 1964)	*
3	Heinrich Hugendubel (1936–2005)	
4	Karl Valentin (Valentin Ludwig Fey) (1882–1948)	
5	Josef Neckermann (1912–1992)	
6	Johann(es) Müller („Regiomontanus“, „der Königsberger“) (1436–1476)	
7	Alexander Dobrindt (* 1970)	
8	Ralph Maria Siegel (1911–1972)	
9	Ernst von Bibra (1806–1878)	
10	Anton Fugger (1493–1560)	
11	Richard Georg Strauss (1864–1949)	
12	Maria Marc (1876–1955)	*
13	Peppi Heiß (* 1963)	
14	Alois Alzheimer (1864–1915)	
15	Friedrich Kaulbach (1912–1992)	
16	Günther Kaufmann (1947–2012)	
17	Roider Jackl (1906–1975)	
18	Irene Epple-Waigel (* 1957)	
19	Dirk Nowitzki (* 1978)	
20	Fritz Koenig (* 1924)	
21	Leopold Prinz von Bayern (* 1943)	
22	Helmut Dietl (* 1944)	
23	Joe Kaeser (Josef Käser) (* 1957)	
24	Christine Neubauer (* 1962)	
25	Robert Müller (1980–2009)	
26	Gabriele Pauli (* 1957)	*
27	Ilse Neubauer (* 1942)	
28	Frank Wörndl (* 1959)	
29	Monika Gruber (* 1971)	
30	Friedrich Zucker (1881–1973)	

Lion Feuchtwanger

Erni Singerl

Martina Gedeck

Rudolph Moshammer

JULI / JULY

1	Robert Lechleiter (* 1980)
2	Monika Hohlmeier (* 1962)
3	Gedeon Burkhard (* 1969)
4	Horst Lorenz Seehofer (* 1949)
5	Sepp Schauer (* 1949)
6	Karin „Muschi“ Stoiber (* 1943)
7	Lion Feuchtwanger (* 1884)
8	Anton Schwarzkopf junior (1924–2001)
9	Hans Jürgen Fahn (* 1952)
10	Carl Orff (1895–1982)
11	Edwin Noël-Baumeister (1944–2004)
12	Simone Melanie Laudehr (* 1986)
13	Thomas Eckart Robert Paulwitz (* 1973)
14	Ruth Drexel (1930–2009)
15	Jürgen Möllemann (1945–2003)
16	Karl Roth (1900–1967)
17	Daniel Brands (* 1987)
18	Fritz Zimmermann (1925–2012)
19	Monika Baumgartner (* 1951)
20	Ludwig Hartmann (* 1978)
21	Helmut Haller (1939–2012)
22	Oskar Maria Graf (1894–1967)
23	Jörg Jaksche (* 1976)
24	Oliver Clemens (* 1968)
25	Franz Engstler (* 1962)
26	Erwin Huber (* 1946)
27	Thomas Gering (* 1958)
28	Ludwig Andreas Feuerbach (1804–1872)
29	Christian Tramitz (* 1955)
30	Reinhard Pappenberger (* 1958)
31	Marcus Grüsser (* 1966)

AUGUST / AUGUST

1	Bastian Schweinsteiger (* 1984)
2	Kathrin Müller-Hohenstein (* 1965)
3	Michael Lerchenberg (* 1953)
4	Florian Silbereisen (* 1981)
5	Doris Schröder-Köpf (* 1963)
6	Johann Andreas Schmeller (1785–1852)
7	Bernd Truntschka (* 1965)
8	Hans Baur (1910–1986)
9	Hubert Haensel (* 1952)
10	Thomas Brunner (* 1962)
11	Andreas Hofmeir (* 1978)
12	Max Straubinger (* 1954)
13	Moritz Bleibtreu (* 1971)
14	Ruth Drexel (* 1930)
15	Johann Nepomuk Mälzel (1772–1838)
16	Matthias Haase (* 1957)
17	Fritz Wepper (* 1941)
18	Harald Greis (* 1976)
19	Wolfgang Grünbauer (* 1965)
20	Veit Wolpert (* 1960)
21	Maximilian Krückl (* 1966)
22	Max Scheler (1874–1928)
23	Bernd Protzner (* 1952)
24	Nina Ruge (* 1956)
25	Ludwig II. Otto Friedrich Wilhelm (1845–1886)
26	Christian Schmidt (* 1957)
27	Marianne Sägebrecht (* 1945)
28	Ad Freundorfer (* 1961)
29	Erni Singerl (1921–2005)
30	Wolfgang Wagner (1919–2010)
31	Magnus Bauch junior (* 1955)

SEPTEMBER / SEPTEMBRE

1	Hermann Albrecht (* 1961)
2	Ina Meling (* 1981)
3	Matthias Klostermayr (1736–1771)
4	Werner Zirngibl (* 1956)
5	Werner Herzog (* 1942)
6	Franz Josef Strauß (1915–1988)
7	Maximilian Steinbeis (* 1970)
8	Markus Babbel (* 1972)
9	Markus Wasmeier (* 1963)
10	Nikolaus Pfanner (* 1956)
11	Franz Anton Beckenbauer (* 1945)
12	Martina Ertl-Renz (* 1973)
13	Maria Furtwängler-Burda (* 1966)
14	Martina Gedeck (* 1961)
15	Charles Schumann (* 1942)
16	Nina Eichinger (* 1981)
17	Robert Lembke (1913–1989)
18	Johanna Uekermann (* 1987)
19	Wolfgang Lackerschmid (* 1956)
20	Richard Stücklen (* 1916 - 2002)
21	Joachim Hermann (* 1956)
22	Fritz Fischer (* 1956)
23	Silvia Seidel (1969–2012)
24	Uschi Obermaier (* 1946)
25	Karl-Heinz Rummenigge (* 1955) *
26	Andreas Scheuer (* 1974)
27	Rudolph Moshammer (1940–2005)
28	Edmund Stoiber (* 1941)
29	Jutta Ditfurth (* 1951)
30	Andreas Ertl (* 1975)

Christian Ude

Gisela Schneeberger

Sisi

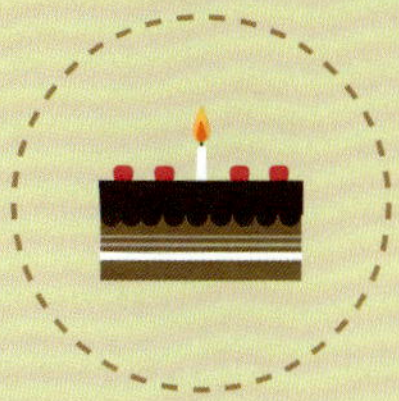

OKTOBER / OCTOBRE

1	Alfons Goppel (1905–1991)	
2	Herbert Riehl-Heyse (1940–2003)	
3	Gisela Schneeberger (* 1948)	
4	Viktoria Rebensburg (* 1989)	
5	Florian Mayer (* 1983)	
6	Adolf Ritter von Hildebrand (1847–1921)	
7	Siegfried „Sigi“ Zimmerschied (* 1953)	
8	Maxi Herber (1920–2006)	
9	Nonnosus Brand (1755–1793)	
10	Xherdan Shaqiri (* 1991)	*
11	Werner Dollinger (1918–2008)	
12	Hanns Seidel (1901–1961)	
13	Bruno Kramm (* 1967)	
14	Michael Althen (1962–2011)	
15	Rudolf von Marogna-Redwitz (1886–1944)	
16	Philipp Kohlschreiber (* 1983)	
17	Adelgunde von Bayern (1870–1958)	
18	Ludwig III.	
19	Mathilde „Hilde“ Gerg (* 1975)	
20	Ernst Hannawald (* 1959)	
21	Udo Wachtveitl (* 1958)	
22	Willibald von Eichstätt (um 700–um 787)	*
23	Amalie von Sachsen-Coburg und Gotha (1848–1894)	*
24	Ludwig Seidel (1821–1896)	*
25	Jannik Inselkammer (1968–2014)	
26	Christian Ude (* 1947)	
27	Wolfgang Aigner (1745–1801)	
28	Heinrich III. (1017–1056)	*
29	Charlotte Knobloch (* 1932)	
30	Anton Gogeisl (1701–1771)	
31	Otto Wiesheu (* 1944)	

NOVEMBER / NOVEMBRE

1	Georg Philipp Harsdörffer (1607–1658)	
2	Nicki (* 1966)	
3	Gerd Müller (* 1945)	
4	Günter Bernard (* 1939)	
5	Hans Sachs (* 1494–1576)	
6	Wolfgang Bischof (* 1960)	
7	Gustl Mollath (* 1956)	
8	Hannsheinz Ports (1922–2010)	
9	Schorsch Meier (1910–1999)	
10	Michaela Gerg-Leitner (* 1965)	
11	Philipp Lahm (* 1983)	
12	Michael Ende (1929–1995)	
13	Daphne Wagner (* 1946)	
14	Leopold Mozart (1719–1787)	
15	Claus Philipp Maria Schenk Graf von Stauffenberg (1907–1944)	
16	Amelie Kober (* 1987)	
17	Elisabeth „Ellis“ Kaut (* 1920)	*
18	Klaus Heinrich Thomas Mann (1906–1949)	
19	Heinrich XIII. (1235–1290)	
20	Wolfgang Stark (* 1969)	
21	Werner Lorant (* 1948)	*
22	Roland Berger (* 1937)	*
23	Günther Beckstein (* 1943)	
24	Maria Höfl-Riesch (* 1984)	
25	Hans Brener (1938–1998)	*
26	Stefan Mross (* 1975)	
27	Günther Grünwald (* 1956)	
28	Armin Bittner (* 1964)	
29	Stefan Bradl (* 1989)	
30	Robert Lohr (* 1966)	

* **Zuagroaste „Bayern“** / Naturalised "Bavarians"

DEZEMBER / DICEMBRE

1	Manfred Köhnlechner (1925–2002)	*
2	Lisa Kreuzer (* 1949)	
3	Bruno Jonas (* 1952)	
4	Jean-Marie Pfaff (* 1953)	*
5	Werner Karl Heisenberg (1901–1976)	
6	Wolf Siegfried Wagner (* 1943)	
7	Ilse Aigner (* 1964)	
8	Susanne Riesch (* 1987)	
9	Wolfgang Fierek (* 1950)	
10	Johann Georg Seidenbusch (1641–1729)	
11	Anton von Perfall (1853–1912)	
12	Liesl Karlstadt (1892–1960)	
13	Curd Gustav Andreas Gottlieb Franz Jürgens (1915–1982)	
14	Michael Glos (* 1944)	
15	Peter Schmidhuber (* 1931)	
16	Johanna Schubert (* 1963)	
17	Theodor von Zwehl (1800–1875)	
18	Walter Otto Hieber (1895–1976)	*
19	Rudolf Hell (1901–2002)	
20	Bruni Löbel (1920–2006)	*
21	Uwe Dick (* 1942)	
22	Bernd Schuster (* 1959)	*
23	Hubert Glaser (* 1928)	
24	Elisabeth Amalie Eugenie („Sisi“) (1837–1898)	
25	Albert Betz (1885–1968)	
26	Jakob Friedrich Binder (1787–1856)	
27	Jakob „Papa“ Geis (1840–1908)	*
28	Franzl Lang (* 1928)	
29	Ludwig Huber (1928–2003)	
30	Alexander Huber (Huber-Buam) (* 1968)	
31	Traudl Hächer (* 1962)	

So soll es sein
What shall be, shall be

Prognosen für den Freistaat, oder wie Karl Valentin schon sagte: *„Die Zukunft war früher auch besser."* / Forecasts for Bavaria or, as Karl Valentin once said: *"The future just isn't what it used to be."*

–1.400
Fehlende Hausärzte bis 2020
Shortage of family doctors by 2020

–90.000
Fehlendes Pflegepersonal bis 2030
Shortage of care personnel by 2030

34 %
Anteil der über 60-Jährigen im Jahr 2029
Ratio of persons over 60 in 2029

46,4 **Jahre** / years
Durchschnittsalter 2029
Average age in 2029

79,7 **Jahre** / years **84,4** **Jahre** / years
Lebenserwartung 2029
Life expectancy by 2029

30 %
Angestrebter Anteil erneuerbarer Energien an der Stromerzeugung 2020
Targeted ratio of renewable energies used for electricity generation by 2020

Atomausstieg abgeschlossen bis 2022
(nach Stilllegung des Atommeilers Isar II)
Nuclear phase-out completed by 2022
(after shutdown of Isar II nuclear power station)

→ 2100

+4 bis / to **6 °C**
im Winter / in winter

+3 bis / to **5 °C**
im Sommer / in summer

Temperaturanstieg in den Alpen bis 2100
Temperature rise in the Alps by 2100

→ 2040

+1,5 %
pro Jahr / per year

Wirtschaftswachstum bis 2040
Economic growth by 2040

Bevölkerungsentwicklung in den kreisfreien Städten und Landkreisen Bayerns
Population development in Bavaria's counties and independent cities
Veränderung 2032 gegenüber 2012
Changes between 2012 and 2032

2012 → 2032

stark abnehmend
decreasing strongly

abnehmend / decreasing

stabil / stable

zunehmend / increasing

stark zunehmend
increasing strongly

→ 2020

Prognose für die fünf bayerischen Gletscher für 2020
Forecast for the five Bavarian glaciers for 2020

geschmolzen / melted

Ergebnisse der letzten Landtagswahl (2013)
Results of the last parliamentary elections (2013)
- **47,7 % CSU** / Christian Social Union
- **20,6 % SPD** / Social Democratic Party
- **9,0 % Freie Wähler** / Free Voters
- **8,6 % Grüne** / The Greens
- **3,3 % FDP** / Free Democratic Party
- **2,1 % Linke** / The Left
- **2,1 % Bayernpartei** / Bavaria Party
- **2,0 % ÖDP** / Ecological Democratic Party
- **4,6 % Sonstige** / Others

Frischgebackene bayerische Mütter
New Bavarian mothers
- **74% stillen** / nurse their babies
- **26 % geben Fläschchen** / bottle-feed

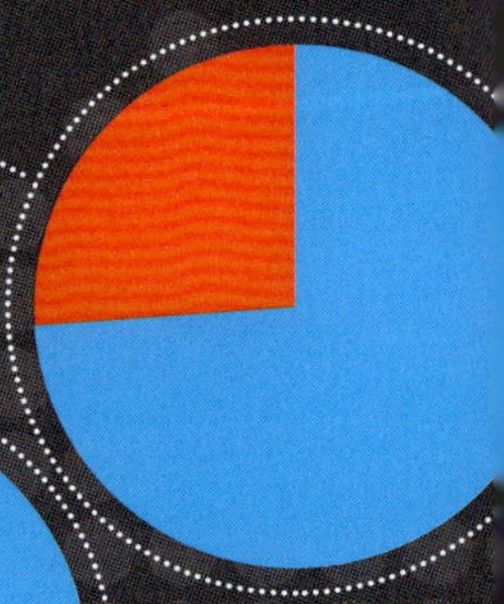

Das letzte Stück
The last piece

Sie wissen immer noch nicht total alles über Bayern? Vielleicht beantwortet dieses Torten-Pichelsteiner die letzten offenen Fragen. / You still don't know everything there is to know about Bavaria? Perhaps this Pichelsteiner stew of pie charts will answer your last remaining questions.

Umfrage im Freistaat: Fühlen Sie sich eher als Bayer oder als Deutscher?
Survey taken in Bavaria: Do you feel more like a Bavarian or a German?
- **54 % Bayer** / Bavarian
- **46 % Deutscher** / German

Prostitution in bayerischen Gemeinden
Prostitution in Bavarian municipalities
- **in 34 (1,7 %) grundsätzlich erlaubt**
  generally permitted
- **in 2.022 (98,3 %) grundsätzlich verboten**
  generally prohibited

Einsatzzeit von Bayern Münchens Torhüter Sepp Maier und seinen Stellvertretern in den Jahren 1964–1978
Playing time for Bayern München's goalkeeper Sepp Maier and his substitutes in the years 1964–1978
- **42.487 Minuten für Sepp Maier**
  minutes for Sepp Maier
- **353 Minuten für die Ersatzmänner**
  minutes for his substitutes

Mitglieder des Ostbayerischen Bart- und Schnauzerclubs
Members of the East Bavaria Beard and Moustache Club
- **77,5 % männlich** / male
- **22,5 % weiblich** / female

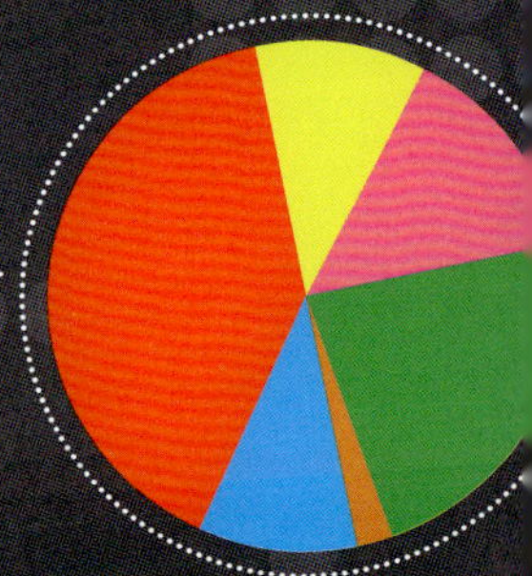

Zutaten Leberkäse / Meat loaf ingredients
- **10 % Rindfleisch** / beef
- **40 % Schweinefleisch** / pork
- **11 % Schweinebacken** / pork cheek
- **14 % Speck** / bacon
- **23 % Eis und Wasser** / ice and water
- **2 % Nitritpökelsalz** / nitrite curing salt

Rollen Gerhard Polts auf seinem Album „Die Klassiker“
Roles played by Gerhard Polt on his album "The Classics"
- **33 % bayerisch (als Mann)** / Bavarian (as man)
- **38 % bayerisch (als Frau)** / Bavarian (as woman)
- **7 % hochdeutsch (als Mann)** / High German (as man)
- **7 % hochdeutsch (als Frau)** / High German (as woman)
- **2 % rülpsend** / burping
- **2 % hustend** / coughing
- **2% als Kind** / as child
- **2% als Schweizer** / as Swiss
- **2% als Österreicher** / as Austrian
- **5% instrumental** / instrumental

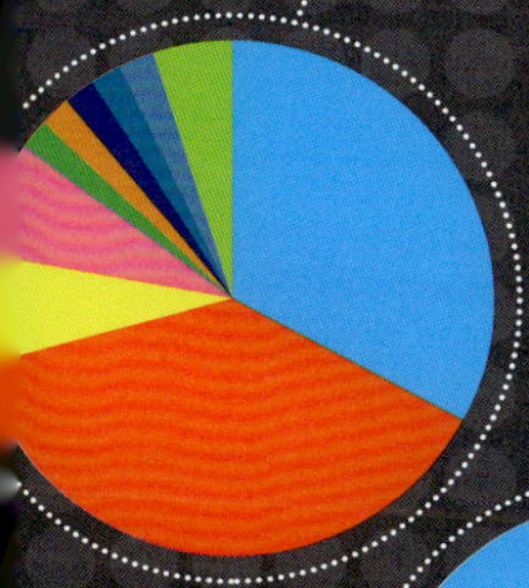

Landeshaushalt / State budget 2013
47.376,3 Mio. / mil. €
Ausgaben in Mio. € / Expenditures in mil. €
- **8.509,9**
  Allgemeine Dienste (u. a. Polizei und Rechtsschutz)
  General services (incl. police and legal protection)
- **17.318,9**
  Bildungswesen, Wissenschaft, Forschung, kulturelle Angelegenheiten
  Education, sciences, research, cultural affairs
- **4.163,5**
  Soziales, Familien, Jugend, Arbeitsmarkt
  Social services, families, youth, job market
- **1.232,7**
  Gesundheit, Umwelt, Sport und Erholung
  Health, environment, sport and recreation
- **417,3**
  Wohnungswesen, Städtebau, Raumordnung und kommunale Gemeinschaftsdienste
  Housing, urban development, land use planning and community services
- **1.027,9**
  Ernährung, Landwirtschaft und Forsten
  Food, agriculture and forestry
- **804,2**
  Energie- und Wasserwirtschaft, Gewerbe, Dienstleistungen
  Energy and water supply, trade and industry, services
- **2.493,4**
  Verkehrs- und Nachrichtenwesen
  Transport and news
- **11.408,5**
  Finanzwirtschaft
  Finance

Schreibweisen des B-Wortes in der deutschen Presse seit 2004
Spelling of the B-word in the German press since 2004
- **5 % bairisch**
- **2 % bayrisch**
- **93 % bayerisch**

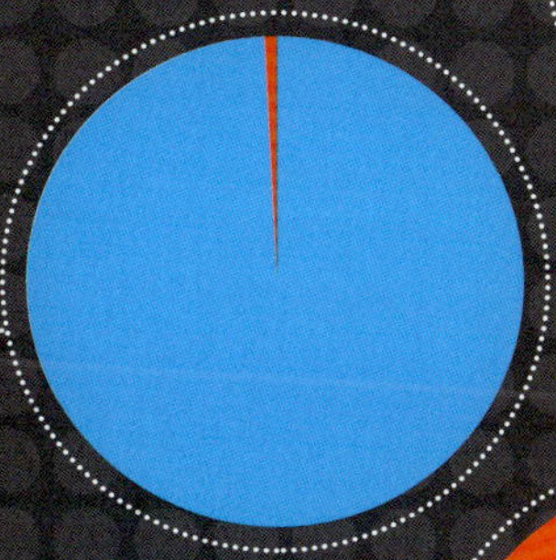

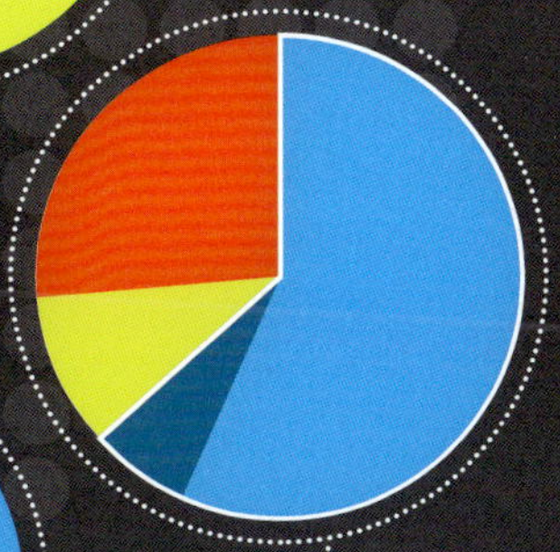

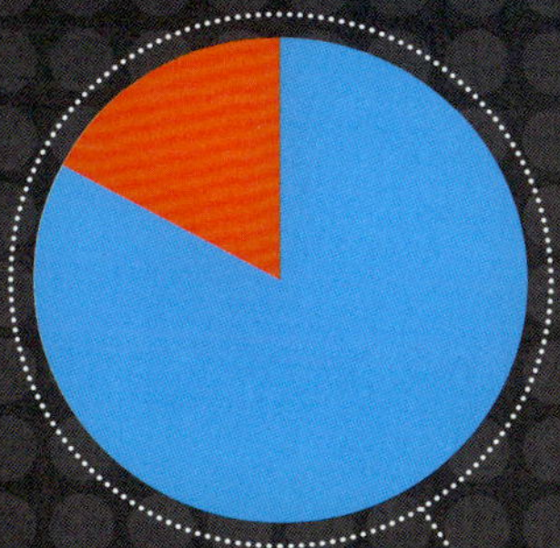

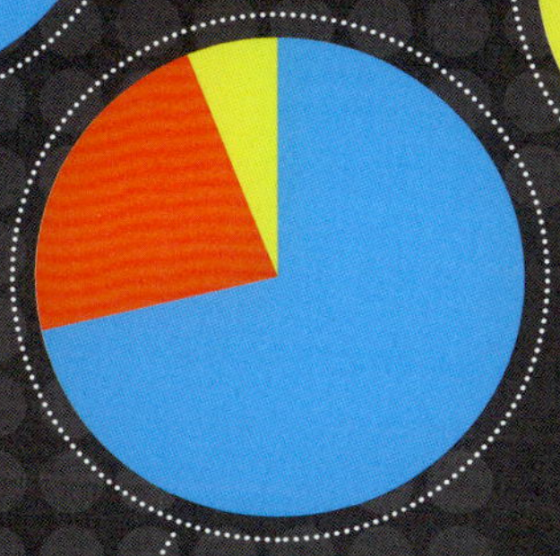

Uferlänge des Bodensees
Lake Constance shoreline
- **173 km in Deutschland** / Germany
  davon / thereof
  - **155 km in Baden-Württemberg**
  - **18 km in Bayern** / Bavaria
- **28 km in Österreich** / Austria
- **72 km in der Schweiz** / Switzerland

„Mariä Himmelfahrt“
Feast of the Assumption (15.8.)
- **82,9 % gesetzlicher Feiertag in 1.704 von insgesamt 2.056 Gemeinden**
  bank holiday in 1,704 of the total 2,056 municipalities

Umfrage: In psychischer Behandlung …
Survey: In psychiatric treatment …
- **71,8 % … war ich noch nie**
  … I have never been
- **22,5 % … war sich schon einmal**
  … I was once
- **5,9 % … bin ich derzeit**
  … I am currently

Quellen
References

8
Eigene Recherche / The authors' own research

10
Bayerisches Landesamt für Statistik und Datenverarbeitung, Statistisches Jahrbuch für Bayern 2013 • Bayerisches Landesamt für Statistik und Datenverarbeitung, www.statistik.bayern.de

12
Bayerisches Landesamt für Statistik und Datenverarbeitung, Statistisches Jahrbuch für Bayern 2013

14
Bayerisches Landesamt für Statistik und Datenverarbeitung, Statistisches Jahrbuch für Bayern 2013

16
Kirchinger, Johann: Der nicht kontrollierbare Raum. Die Deutung der bäuerlichen Arbeitswelt in der Moderne – im Spiegel der Eigennamen für Nutztiere. In: Beiträge zur Namenforschung 50 (2014) • Klausmann, Hubert: Atlas der Familiennamen von Bayern. Ostfildern: Thorbecke 2009 • Knud Bielefeld, www.beliebte-vornamen.de

18
Antenne Bayern GmbH & Co. KG, www.antenne.de • Aventura do Brasil Viagens Ltda. ME, www.aventuradobrasil.de • Google Maps, https://maps.google.com • Neumann, Jürgen / Prokopetz, Johannes. Bayerns lustigste Ortsnamen. Frankfurt/Main: Societätsverlag 2010 • Sambaco GmbH, www.samba-festival.de • www.nachrichten.at

20
Bayerisches Landesamt für Statistik und Datenverarbeitung, Statistisches Jahrbuch für Bayern 2013

22
Bayerischer Jagdverband e. V., www.jagd-bayern.de • Bayerisches Landesamt für Statistik und Datenverarbeitung, Statistisches Jahrbuch für Bayern 2013 • Eigene Recherche / The authors' own research

24
Renn, Manfred / König, Werner: Kleiner Bayerischer Sprachatlas. München: dtv 2009

26
Stephan Straßer, Gehörlosenverband München und Umland e. V., www.gmu.de

28
Bayerisches Landesamt für Statistik und Datenverarbeitung, Statistisches Jahrbuch für Bayern 2013 • Meintz, René, www.kirchenaustritt.de • Spiegel online GmbH, www.spiegel.de • Stadt Altötting, www.altoetting.de • www.autobild.de

30
Bayerisches Landesamt für Statistik und Datenverarbeitung, Statistisches Jahrbuch für Bayern 2013 • Bayerisches Staatsministerium des Innern, für Bau und Verkehr, www.stmi.bayern.de

32
Ärzte Zeitung online, www.aerztezeitung.de • Bayerische Staatszeitung, www.bayerische-staatszeitung.de • Bayerisches Staatsministerium für Arbeit und Soziales, Familie und Integration • Bayerisches Staatsministerium für Gesundheit und Pflege • BÖLW, Bund Ökologische Lebensmittelwirtschaft e. V., www.boelw.de • dpa, Deutsche Presse-Agentur GmbH, www.dpa.de • Frankfurter Allgemeine Zeitung GmbH, www.faz.de • INSM-Initiative Neue Soziale Marktwirtschaft GmbH, www.bundeslaenderranking.de • Playboy Deutschland Publishing GmbH, www.playboy.de • Statista GmbH, http://de.statista.com • stern.de GmbH, www.stern.de • Süddeutsche Zeitung, www.sueddeutsche.de • www.kliniken.de

34
Bayerisches Landesamt für Statistik und Datenverarbeitung, Statistisches Jahrbuch für Bayern 2013 • Bayerisches Landesamt für Statistik und Datenverarbeitung, www.statistik.bayern.de

36
Haus der Bayerischen Geschichte, München, www.hdbg.de • Wikipedia

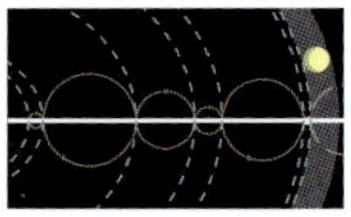

38
Christlich-Soziale Union in Bayern e. V., www.csu.de • Wikipedia

40
Council on Tall Buildings and Urban Habitat, The Skyscraper Center, http://skyscrapercenter.com • Wikipedia • www.muenchen.de • www.youtube.com/watch?v=FW6P_crgp8M

42
Baumann, Franziska: Wandern am Wasser Bayerische Alpen: Bergseen, Schluchten und Wildbäche. Oberhaching: Rother 2013 • Bayerischer Rundfunk, www.br.de • bergfex GmbH, www.bergfex.de • Bergsteiger, www.bergsteiger.de • Bergwacht Bayern, www.bergwacht-bayern.de • Deutscher Alpenverein, www.alpenverein.de • Süddeutsche Zeitung, www.sueddeutsche.de • Wikipedia • WWF Deutschland, www.wwf.de

44
Augsburger Allgemeine Zeitung, www.augsburger-allgemeine.de • Bayerisches Landesamt für Statistik und Datenverarbeitung, Statistisches Jahrbuch für Bayern 2013 • Bayerisches Landesamt für Umwelt, www.lfu.bayern.de • Konradin Medien GmbH, www.wissen.de

46
Bayerische Landesanstalt für Wald und Forstwirtschaft, www.lwf.bayern.de • Bayerisches Staatsministerium für Ernährung, Landwirtschaft und Forsten, www.stmelf.bayern.de

48
Bayerischer Jagdverband e. V., www.jagd-bayern.de • Wikipedia

50
Eigene Recherche / The authors' own research

52
Eigene Recherche / The authors' own research

54
Bayerische Landesanstalt für Landwirtschaft, www.lfl.bayern.de • Bayerisches Landesamt für Statistik und Datenverarbeitung, Statistisches Jahrbuch für Bayern 2013 • Statista GmbH, http://de.statista.com • Statistisches Bundesamt, www.destatis.de

56
KErn, Kompetenzzentrum für Ernährung, Kulmbach, www.kern.bayern.de • Max-Rubner-Institut / Bundesforschungsinstitut für Ernährung und Lebensmittel (Hrsg.): Nationale Verzehrsstudie II, 2008, www.bmel.de • Statistisches Bundesamt, Mikrozensus 2009, www.destatis.de

58
Bayerisches Staatsministerium für Ernährung, Landwirtschaft und Forsten, Spezialitätendatenbank, www.spezialitaetenland-bayern.de

60
Metzgerei Magnus Bauch, München, http://mbwassonst.de

62
Allianz Arena München Stadion GmbH, www.allianz-arena.de • Bayerischer Brauereibund e. V., www.bayrisch-bier.de • Bayerisches Landesamt für Statistik und Datenverarbeitung, www.statistik.bayern.de • Focus Magazin Verlag GmbH, www. focus.de • München Betriebs-GmbH & Co. KG, www.muenchen.de • Statista GmbH, http://de.statista.com • Wikipedia

64
Arte G.E.I.E., www.arte.tv • Eigene Recherche / The authors' own research • Wikipedia

66
Eigene Recherche / The authors' own research

68
Gesellschaft für Nachrichten und Zeitgeschehen mbH, www.n24.de • Statista GmbH, http://de.statista.com • www.oktoberfest.de

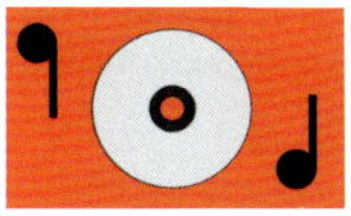

70
Bayerische Blasmusikverband e. V., www.bbmv-online.de • Die Münchner Philharmoniker, www.mphil.de • Eigene Recherche / The authors' own research • LaBrassBanda, www.labrassbanda.com • Münchner Zwietracht, www.muenchnerzwietracht.de • ProSiebenSat.1 Digital GmbH, www.prosieben.de • Regensburger Domspatzen, www.domspatzen.de • Spider Murphy Gang, www.spider-murphy-gang.de

72
Beekmann, Kai, www.bayerische-kultserien.de • Eigene Recherche / The authors' own research • IMDb.com, Inc., www.imdb.com • Wikipedia

74
Frankfurter Allgemeine Zeitung GmbH, www.faz.de • Hamburger Morgenpost, www.mopo.de • Quotenmeter GmbH, www.quotenmeter.de • RP Digital GmbH, www.rp-online.de • Wikipedia • www.dwdl.de • Zweites Deutsches Fernsehen, ZDF Jahrbuch, www.zdf-jahrbuch.de

76
Bayreuther Festspiele GmbH, www.bayreuther-festspiele.de • Focus Magazin Verlag GmbH, www.focus.de • Handelsblatt GmbH, www.handelsblatt.com • Spiegel online GmbH, www.spiegel.de • stern.de GmbH, www.stern.de • Süddeutsche Zeitung, www.sueddeutsche.de • Wikipedia

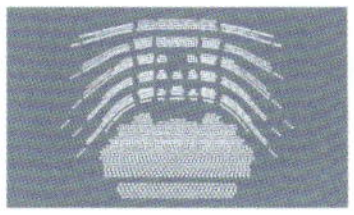

78
Bayerisches Landesamt für Statistik und Datenverarbeitung, Statistisches Jahrbuch für Bayern 2013 • Bayerisches Staatsministerium für Bildung und Kultur, Wissenschaft und Kunst • Bayerische Staatsoper, www.bayerische.staatsoper.de • Süddeutsche Zeitung, www.sueddeutsche.de • Verband bayerischer Amateurtheater e. V., www.amateurtheater-bayern.de

80
Audi AG, Audi MediaServices, www.audimediaservices.com • Bayerisches Landesamt für Statistik und Datenverarbeitung, Statistisches Jahrbuch für Bayern 2013 • Bayerische Motoren Werke AG, BMW Welt, www.bmw-welt.com

82
Bayerische Verwaltung der staatlichen Schlösser, Gärten und Seen, www.schloesser.bayern.de • Bayerischer Rundfunk, www.br.de • Bernstein, Martin (Hrsg.): Berge, Schlösser, Königsträume – Auf den Spuren König Ludwigs II. Süddeutsche Zeitung Edition 2011 • Staffelsee-Gymnasium Murnau, Kulturpfad Ludwig II., http://ludwig.cmswp.de • Wikipedia

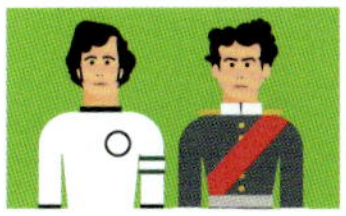

84
Bayerische Verwaltung der staatlichen Schlösser, Gärten und Seen, www.neuschwanstein.de • Haus der Bayerischen Geschichte, München, www.hdbg.de • Süddeutsche Zeitung, www.sueddeutsche.de • Stiftung Haus der Geschichte der Bundesrepublik Deutschland, www.hdg.de • Wikipedia

86
11FREUNDE Verlag GmbH & Co. KG, www.11freunde.de • Draxler, Alfred / Beckenbauer, Franz: 40 Jahre Bundesliga. Berlin: Ullstein 2003 • FC Bayern München AG, www.fcbayern.de • Handelsblatt GmbH, www.handelsblatt.com • Herold, Frank, www.marketing-blog.biz • RP Digital GmbH, www.rp-online.de • The Brand Finance Institute, www.brandfinance.com • Transfermarkt GmbH & Co. KG, www.transfermarkt.de • Wikipedia

88
Bayerischer Fußball-Verband e. V., www.bfv.de • Biermann, Christoph / Köster, Philipp: Fast alles über 50 Jahre Bundesliga. Köln: Kiepenheuer & Witsch 2013 • Deutscher Fußball-Bund e. V., www.dfb.de • DFL, Deutsche Fußball Liga GmbH, www.bundesliga.de • Süddeutsche Zeitung, www.sueddeutsche.de • Wikipedia

90
Adidas Geschäftsbericht, www.adidas-group.com • Handelsblatt GmbH, www.handelsblatt.com • Nike Annual Report, http://investors.nikeinc.com • Puma Annual Report, www.puma-annual-report.com • Wikipedia • www.nurfussball.com • www.wm-trikots.org

92
Angerer, Nadine, www.angerer-nadine.de • Antenne Bayern GmbH & Co. KG, www.antenne.de • Bundesministerium der Finanzen, www.zoll.de • Friesinger, Anni, www.anni-friesinger.de • Schaffelhuber, Anna, www.annaschaffelhuber.de • Theiss, Christine, www.christinetheiss.de • Wikipedia

94
Bayerischer Rundfunk, www.br.de • dpa, Deutsche Presse-Agentur GmbH, www.dpa.de • Hochschule für angewandte Wissenschaften – Hochschule Ansbach, www.jupo-bayern.de • Neue Presse Multimedia GmbH, www.heimatzeitung.de • Siemens AG, www.siemens.com • Wikipedia

96
ADAC e. V., www.adac.de • Bayerisches Landesamt für Statistik und Datenverarbeitung, www.statistik.bayern.de • Bayerisches Landesamt für Statistik und Datenverarbeitung, Statistisches Jahrbuch für Bayern 2013 • Bayerischer Rundfunk, www.br.de • Spiegel online GmbH, www.spiegel.de • VDMA, Verband Deutscher Maschinen- und Anlagenbau e. V., www.vdma.org • Wikipedia

98
Audi AG, www.audi.de • Eigene Recherche / The authors' own research

100
BMW Group, www.bmwgroup.com • Wikipedia

102
Bayerisches Landesamt für Statistik und Datenverarbeitung, Statistisches Jahrbuch für Bayern 2013 • Eigene Recherche / The authors' own research

104
Allgäu Airport – Flughafen Memmingen, www.allgaeu-airport.de • Flightradar24, www.flightradar24.com • Flughafen München „Franz Josef Strauß", www.munich-airport.de • Flughafen Nürnberg, www.airport-nuernberg.de • Wikipedia

106
Abendzeitung München, www.abendzeitung-muenchen.de • Allianz Arena München Stadion GmbH, www.allianz-arena.de • Alois Dallmayr KG, www.dallmayr-versand.de • Alphornbau Alois Biermaier, Bischofswiesen, www.alphornbau-biermaier.de • Bayerisches Landesamt für Statistik und Datenverarbeitung, Statistisches Jahrbuch für Bayern 2013 • Bayerische Seenschifffahrt GmbH, www.seenschifffahrt.de • Bayreuther Festspiele GmbH, https://ticketshop.bayreuther-festspiele.de • Bergwacht Bayern, www.bergwacht-bayern.de • Bootsverleih Stöffl, Prien am Chiemsee, www.stoeffl.de • Deutsche Bahn AG, www.bahn.com • Donaukurier Ingolstadt, www.donaukurier.de • Feinkost Käfer, München, http://shop.feinkost-kaefer.de • Immowelt AG, http://presse.immowelt.de • Lederhosen Stangassinger, Berchtesgaden, www.lederhosen-macher.com • Münchner Merkur, www.merkur-online.de • Münchner Wochenanzeiger, www.wochenanzeiger-muenchen.de • Süddeutsche Zeitung, www.sueddeutsche.de • Tourismus Oberstdorf, www.oberstdorf.de • Transfermarkt GmbH & Co. KG, www.transfermarkt.de • www.amazon.de • www.cinemaxx.de • www.muenchen.de • Zur Aubinger Einkehr, www.aubinger-einkehr-muenchen.de

108
Eigene Recherche / The authors' own research

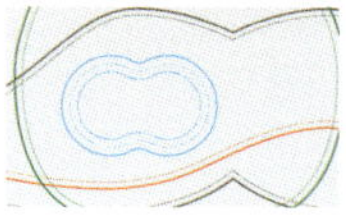

110
Bartclub Regenstauf, www.bartclub-regenstauf-2009.de • Bayerischer Rundfunk, www.br.de • Bayerische Staatszeitung, www.bayerische-staatszeitung.de • Joint Forces Media GmbH, www.basketball.de • Playmobil®, www.playmobil.de •

112
Bayerische Vermessungsverwaltung, http://vermessung.bayern.de • Bayerisches Landesamt für Statistik und Datenverarbeitung, Statistisches Jahrbuch für Bayern 2013 • Bayerisches Staatsministerium des Innern, für Bau und Verkehr, www.stmi.bayern.de • Burghauser Touristik GmbH, http://tourismus.burghausen.de • Curd Biedermann Biketouristik, www.bayernbike.de • Füssen Tourismus und Marketing, www.fuessen.de • Google Maps, https://maps.google.com • Nationalpark Bayerischer Wald, www.nationalpark-bayerischer-wald.de • Wikipedia

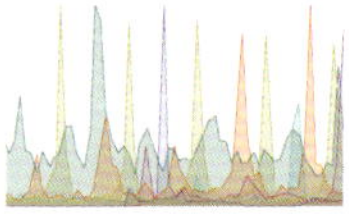

114
Google Trends, www.google.de/trends

118
Eigene Recherche / The authors' own research • Korioth, Daniel, geboren.am, http://geboren.am • Wikipedia

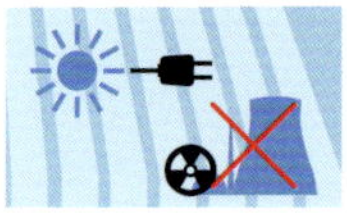

122
Bayerische Landesärztekammer, www.blaek.de • Bayerisches Staatsministerium für Umwelt und Verbraucherschutz, Gletscherbericht, http://www.stmuv.bayern.de • Energie-Atlas Bayern, www.energieatlas.bayern.de • Robert-Koch-Institut, Abteilung für Epidemiologie und Gesundheitsberichterstattung (Hrsg.): Kleinräumige Bedarfsprognosen, 2011 • vbw, Vereinigung der Bayerischen Wirtschaft e. V., http://www.vbw-bayern.de •

124
Bayerisches Landesamt für Gesundheit und Lebensmittelsicherheit, STELLA – Studie zum Ernährungsverhalten im Säuglingsalter, www.lgl.bayern.de • Bayerisches Staatsministerium der Finanzen, für Landesentwicklung und Heimat, www.stmf.bayern.de • Biermann, Christoph / Köster, Philipp: Fast alles über 50 Jahre Bundesliga. Köln: Kiepenheuer & Witsch 2013 • DAK-Gesundheit, www.dak.de • Gruber, Thomas: Ansichtssache Bayern: Annäherungen an eine Heimat, Frankfurter Societäts-Druckerei 2010 • Ostbayerischer Bart- und Schnauzerclub 1996 e. V., www.bcostbayern.de • Polt, Gerhard: Album „Die Klassiker" • Wikipedia